FREEDOM IN EDUCATION

A DO-IT-YOURSELF GUIDE
TO THE LIBERATION OF LEARNING

Libertarian Education is a small independent publishing collective, which for the past quarter of a century has been campaigning for the development of non-authoritarian initiatives in education. As well as books, they publish the termly magazine, *Lib ED*.

Also in this series:

Free School, The White Lion Experience, by Nigel Wright, ISBN 0-9513997-1-3.

Next in this series:

No master, high or low, libertarian education and schooling from 1890 to 1990, by John Shotton, ISBN 0-9513997-3-X.

Freedom

in

Education

**A do-it-yourself guide
to the liberation of learning**

Libertarian Education

Published by:

Libertarian Education
Phoenix House, 170 Wells Road, Bristol, BS4 2AG.

ISBN 0-9513997-2-1

Copyright: Libertarian Education 1992

Printed and bound by:
BPCC Wheatons Ltd., Hennock Road, Marsh Barton, Exeter, EX2
8RP. (Tel: 0392-74121, Fax: 0392-217170)

Photographs:

front cover by (from the top) Ann James, *Lib ED*, Yoshi Nagata,
Lib ED.

page 10: Buktu Learning Centre (*Lib ED*)
page 20: Goldhill Adventure Playground (Terry Morgan)
page 44: courtesy of Ankur, India

Graphics on pages viii and 30 by John Watson.

Contents

Contents

PREFACE

Welcome to *Lib ED*'s second book, *Freedom in Education, a do-it-yourself guide to the liberation of learning.*

Why such a guide? The answer lies in the ever-increasing repression of most educational institutions and the heavy attack that is being made on more open and non-authoritarian approaches to learning. In the 1970s, when right wing educationalists published the 'Black Papers', they were laughed out of court. Only their authors, and their friends and patrons, took them seriously. Now they are all in government, or calling the tune in the Department of Education and Science. Learners young and old are suffering the consequences of their prejudices as the implications of the new education and local government legislation become clear.

Libertarian educational ideas offer a sensible and clear alternative to the current educational ideology. We have included a collection of curriculum articles which introduce practical ideas. Also, we include contact addresses of groups and organisations in Britain and abroad that campaign for aspects of the liberation of learning. An index of articles from *Lib ED* magazine, going back over twenty years, and a wide-ranging bibliography conclude the book.

Lib ED is a termly magazine which examines radical ideas and practice in education. Between issues we produce a newsletter which provides an information exchange for the growing libertarian education network. Both the magazine and the network newsletter focus mainly on Britain, but have an international perspective which reflects a developing exchange of news and ideas between *Lib ED* and our many overseas contacts. Full details can be obtained from: *Lib ED*, Phoenix House, 170 Wells Road, Bristol, BS4 2AG.

We hope that you enjoy *Freedom in Education*, and we welcome as much feedback as possible. The book will be updated regularly, hopefully with the help of our readers, through suggestions for additional articles, material, contacts and resources. We will also be publishing a number of other books looking at other libertarian educational ideas in more depth.

Libertarian Education

A beginner's guide to freedom in education

A sort of pretend interview where you ask really naive questions and we provide interesting, informative answers.

1.   What's wrong with ordinary education anyway?
It is anti-life, it is a systematic attempt to repress the natural instincts of the developing person. Play, fun, spontaneity and love are crushed and replaced by conformity and the fear of freedom.

2.   But some people like it.
Of course ... a lot of ordinary authoritarian education is simply building on the foundations laid by traditional authoritarian child-rearing. Even before entering school the child has been 'broken'. The child's personality develops as a projection of the parent's ambition - the rest is repressed - the child is polite, quiet, guilt-ridden and awaiting further instructions. It's not surprising that many of them want to be told what, when and how to learn.

3.   Well, what's the alternative?
Freedom - freedom for people of all ages to learn what they want, with teachers supporting the learning, not directing it, no matter how subtlely.

4.   Isn't that a bit pie in the sky?
Not at all. It's not only practical but it exists. There are lots of schools and colleges around the world where there is freedom in education. In England Summerhill is probably the best known example.

5.   Are they all fee paying places?
Not entirely. In this country most progressive schools are outside the state system and exist by charging fees, but some like The Sutton Centre in

Nottingham are financed by local authorities. In other countries such as Denmark, the state is more prepared to fund free schools and in those countries there is much less need to charge fees.

6.   Well what of the rest? They won't change will they?
They are already changing, they are becoming more authoritarian. As the economy continues to decline, the state is even less disposed to allow experimentation and creativity in schools. Cost-effectiveness and discipline are the order of the day. The need for the education system to meet the increasingly stringent needs of the state are more and more articulated. What schools do for (or to) the individual is even less considered.

7.   Is there no hope for most state education?
Some - there are positive developments, the emergence of Black and Women's studies, the provision of girl-only spaces, the abolition of the cane, all demonstrate real gains for libertarians.

8.   Is this libertarian idea of education new, then? Has it developed as a critique of modern society?
Yes and no - No it's not new, in that schools have been criticised since they were first invented, but the developed libertarian philosophy of education goes back about 200 years to William Godwin who wrote of the child as "as individual being with powers of reasoning, with sensations of pleasure and pain and with principles of morality ... By the system of

nature he is placed by himself; he has a claim upon his little sphere of empire and discretion; and he is entitled to his appropriate portion of independence." Since then many people, including Tolstoy, Ferrer, A.S. Neill and Paul Goodman have developed the idea. But is is also new in the sense that it continues to develop. We see *Libertarian Education* in that tradition, updating the critique of authoritarian education as we also describe and encourage the libertarian alternative.

9. But if libertarian ideas are so good, why hasn't the education system adopted them?

Mainly because it is in the interests of some people to make sure that institutions don't develop along libertarian lines, people who profit from the willingness of others to be exploited and enjoy it. Most importantly the owners of capital who want workers who will not only work for less than their work gives the owner in profit but who will be grateful for the opportunity. Ultimately, though, so many of us gain a vested interest in the prevailing system that the majority are reluctant, at least initially, to see changes ...

10. How can we support the struggle for libertarian education

Firstly by being critical - by questioning what the experts are telling us, whether the experts are teachers, journalists or parents. It is helpful if we can work in groups with other people in the same position. We can do this as women, kids, teachers, whatever, we don't need a political party. In fact the record of all of the major political parties in Britain on education is bad. The problem is that most parties think they know best how to organise peoples' lives. The libertarian idea is for people to control their own lives.

The struggle will mainly be local and small scale, around issues people feel strongly about. Talking to friends, reading, picketing, writing, organising might all be involved, but in a way

determined by those involved. Our role is to keep people in touch with the positive developments. To inform the struggle and encourage it along. Sometimes we must work in institutions and with people who seem oppressive, but we must try to keep in touch with our own feelings.

Reprinted from *Lib Ed*, Vol 2 No. 1, Spring 1986.

For much more detail, see books listed in the bibliography.

Maths for a change

The structure of traditional Maths teaching reinforces authoritarianism. What can be done about it?

In June '86 school students sitting a London Regional Board CSE Maths examination were asked to carry out the following calculation:

"The money required to provide adequate food, water, education, health and housing for everyone in the world has been estimated at £17 billion a year".
(New Internationalist, 1980)

How many weeks of NATO and Warsaw Pact military spending would be enough to pay for this?

(Show all your working)

This was the final part of a long question which looked at the military expenditure of NATO and Warsaw Pact countries, through graphs, tables and pictograms. Exam entrants were expected to calculate the average percentage rise in spending on arms between 1980 and 1984 for the USA and USSR - answer USA 39%, USSR 7.5%. What is more, they were then asked to comment on this result. Another section called for the student to work out the military spending per head in the UK in 1980.

Not surprisingly, the question caused a stir among certain right-wing educationalists. A spokesperson for the examination board said that they always vetted social science subjects for political bias, but that it had never occurred to them to look at maths. It probably wouldn't occur to many people. Mathematics has a high status as a politically neutral subject, objective and value-free. Does this view of maths stand up to scrutiny?

The examples below are all taken from text-books widely used in schools and colleges today.

A shopgirl works a 46 hour week for which she is paid £58.88. She works four hours overtime which is paid for at time and a quarter. How much did she earn in that week?

A supermarket has 1800 cm² of shelf space for washing powder. A box of Sure-Clean requires 25 cm² of shelf space and a box of Quick-Wash 15 cm². The profit per box is 16p for Sure-Clean and 24p for Quick-Wash. How many boxes of each should be stocked for the greatest profit to be made?

A man borrowed £2400 for 2 years at 11% compound interest. How much will he have to repay?

When an aircraft is flying horizontally at a speed of 420 km/h, it releases a bomb, which on release has the same velocity as the aircraft. The bomb is released when the aircraft is 2 km horizontally and h km vertically from the target. Given that the bomb hits the target, find the value of h.

So what lessons are children learning under the guise of mathematics? Hierarchies are legitimised - some people are paid a fixed monthly salary, while others have to work long hours of overtime to get enough money to live on. The only criterion for decision-making in business is the maximisation of profit, and profit doesn't arise from exploiting people's labour, but is the difference between cost price and selling price. War is an exercise in calculating the trajectories of bombs and bullets, or the number of soldiers needed to storm the radio station during a coup. Most people who do anything of note are men, and all of them are white.

The structure of traditional mathematics teaching, even more than most subjects, reinforces authoritarianism generally. There is only one correct answer to every question, known by the teacher, arrived at not by investigation and discussion, but by applying a formula. In other areas of the curriculum, such as social studies, students may be expected to question and debate the structure of society, but these subjects do not have the high status enjoyed by maths.

So what can a teacher of mathematics do to change the emphasis of the maths classroom away from the legitimisation of capitalism, racism, militarism and sexism? A start has been made - the CSE question about military spending was the product of SMILE (Secondary Mathematics Individualised Learning Experiment). This is a work-card based scheme, originated by London teachers, but now also used in schools outside of London. SMILE questions refer to Krishna, Soulla, Delroy, Ms Sharma and Mr Dabrowski, instead of Tom, Dick and Harry. Girls are not only prominent, but shown to be dynamic and decisive. Other individual teachers and groups are now producing materials which portray black people and women.

For some years progressive teachers have tried to bring a multicultural dimension to maths teaching. Islamic patterns or Hindu rangoli designs can be used to investigate symmetry or tessellations in geometry. Bilingual children can teach others in the class to count in the language they speak at home. If the history of maths is touched on, this can be used to challenge the Eurocentric bias of 'Pascal's Triangle', or 'Pythagoras' Theorem'. We can talk about the great mathematical achievements of the Indians and the Chinese. Pascal's Triangle was used by Chinese mathematicians 300 years before Pascal's birth. The number system that we use today came from India via the Arabs, replacing the inefficient Roman numerals that were the best that Europe had come up with. Children can play mathematical games from around the world, or look at different calendars. There's nothing wrong with this multicultural approach, as far as it goes. It just doesn't go far enough. Mathematics, and especially statistics, can be used to present, in a graphic way, issues related to the global division of wealth, the position of women, apartheid.

A standard text book example of a pie-chart shows the world's land area is divided between the continents, a pretty meaningless exercise. Why not draw two pie-charts to compare the distribution of population with the amount of energy consumed, and then discuss the 'fairness' of this division.

Other ideas for graphs and charts related to world development are infant mortality rates, life expectancy, food imports and exports. 'Aid' can be shown up for the fraud that it is, and the colonialist background to the present economic structure of the world explained. There's the exercise in ratio and percentage: "If there were 100 ...". For example:

If there were 100 people in the world, this is where they would be

Africa	9
East Europe and U.S.S.R.	9
East Asia	34
Latin America	8
North America	6
Oceania	1
South Asia	20
West Asia	3
Western Europe	10

If there were 100 banknotes in the world, this is where they would be

Africa	3
East Europe and U.S.S.R.	18
East Asia	14
Latin America	5
North America	28
Oceania	1
South Asia	2
West Asia	2
Western Europe	27

Another area is the position of women globally. It has been estimated that women perform two thirds of the world's work hours, receive 10% of the world's income, and own 1% of the world's property. Would the figures for Britain agree with this?

Then there's the vegetarian alternative. 10 acres of land will support:

60 people growing soya
24 people growing wheat
10 people growing maize
2 people growing cattle

Charities like Oxfam, Christian Aid and War on Want, and the magazine New Internationalist, are good sources of information.

We have seen how SMILE used statistics on arms spending. There is a wealth of figures to look at here. For example, compare the money spent on health with military spending for different countries or areas of the world. How much does a Cruise Missile cost? What else could you buy for the same money? How many times over would everybody in the world be killed by the nuclear weapons in existence now?

South Africa's apartheid system provides a huge amount of statistical information for use in a maths lesson to bring home the realities of institutionalised racism. Compare the infant mortality rate for white babies (18.6 per ,000) with that for black babies (112.2 per ,000). Or what about a bar chart to show the per capita spending on education for the different 'racial' groups (the whites got more than 7 times as much as the blacks in 1982/3). Then there's a pie chart to illustrate the exports from South Africa to various parts of the world in 1982 (13.7% came to Britain).

Under apartheid 15% of the population (the whites) have taken for themselves 87% of the land. In a group of 20 children, this would mean that 3 children had almost all the classroom for their own use and crowded the other 17 into a corner. Racism in Britain can be tackled too - for instance comparing the figures for black people picked up on Sus with the number actually charged. Other possible areas to look at are housing and unemployment.

This isn't only an excuse for introducing information about apartheid, or world trade, or arms spending, into a maths class. The thinking and talking that will go on about these issues should also change the way in which children relate to maths. Instead of an oppressive, meaningless set of operations about nothing at all, mathematics can be a powerful tool for interpreting the world. Mathematical thinking can be used to look at real problems, demystifying the economic and social structures that surround us. If this starts to happen, then students may begin to see some point in learning maths for a change.

Reprinted from *Lib Ed*, Vol. 2 No. 4, Spring 1987.

RESOURCES

Organisations

Christian Aid, PO Box 100, London, SE1 7RT.
New Internationalist (subscription office), FREEPOST, Mitcham, Surrey, CR4 9AR.
Oxfam Youth and Education Department, 274 Banbury Road, Oxford, OX2 8DX.
Radical Statistics Group, 9 Poland Street, London, SW1.
War on Want, 37-39 Great Guidford Street, London, SE1 0ES.

Publications

Everyone counts, ILEA, 1985.
Making Sense of Statistics, Steve Johnson (Tressell Publications, 1985)
Mathematics For All, Wiltshire Education Authority, 1987
Relearning Mathematics: a different third R - radical Maths, by Marilyn Frankenstein, Free Association Books, 1989.

Global Statistics (computer software package), Centre for Global Education, University of York, York, YO1 5DD.

Alternative futures now!

The future is something that always seems to be confined to science fiction. Here David Hicks looks at alternative futures, and the need to educate and plan for their development.

"Wherever I look", said a friend, "I keep seeing the word 'future'. It's just another fad". Well, it does seem as if the last decade of a century prompts more widespread speculation than usual about the future, but this is no bad thing as we approach the third millenium AD.

We need to look at, and to think about, alternative futures, not least because there has been a growing consensus for some time that humankind is at a major turning point. As we face problems of global warming, with its consequent potential for mass disruption of human affairs, there is increasing uncertainty both about what sort of future we want, and what we might get.

Because issues to do with future often seem intangible and unknowable, and because this may create anxiety, then teachers often feel that it is not a legitimate area to explore with students. Yet it is essential that we do for, to rephrase George Orwell, "He who owns the present, will control the future".

There are two main ways in which the future can be 'colonised'. Firstly, adults directly and indirectly try to control children's images of the future, both through the media and through their own more limited ways of thinking and being. Thus, from an early age, children will have had their thinking about tomorrow's possibilities diminished. A range of potential futures may therefore have already vanished from possible consciousness.

We steal the birthright of the young in order to impose our own more limited and sanitised visions. Many children thus learn to become docile consumers, their images of the future often unwitting parodies of the 'ethnocratic/consumerist dream'.

Secondly, many 'experts' on the future take the existing socio- political status quo as a 'given', and thereby promote images of the future which merely serve to perpetuate the global economic inequalities of the present. Based, as they often are, on mechanistic, technocratic and patriarchal assumptions, such scenarios, it can be argued, merely "colonise the future" on behalf of existing elites.

We need to help children explore a range of alternative futures because, in times of rapid change such as ours, anticipatory skills become essential for survival. Whilst the school curriculum tends to be embedded in the past, it is enacted in the present and, at least theoretically, is orientated towards the future. Thus all approaches to education make some assumptions about the future, even though it is often that the future will be much like, or a glossier version of, today.

Teaching about the future is therefore not just about being fashionable, but has, rather, a clear educational rationale. In Rick Slaughter's words, "We cannot alter the past, but we have common interests in achieving life-preserving, sustainable future.

It follows that a central task for teachers is to explore with their pupils some of the major problems and possibilities that lie ahead, and therefore sensitise them to the implications of choices and actions in the present ... The 'future' assumes new meaning when we realise that we cannot 'opt out'. All actions and choices (including choices *not* to act or choose) have consequences".

Our lives are constantly shaped by images of the future, whether of what we hope will happen tomorrow or of our plans for the next year. If, however, we are not fully aware of the options open to us, both in our personal lives and globally, then our choices are made on insufficient and inadequate evidence.

Teaching and learning about the future can thus help students to become more flexible and adaptable, to be pro-active rather than re-active to change. It can also help develop critical thinking skills and the creative imagination, be a spur to personal achievement and help to develop a sense of responsible and co-operative global citizenship.

Much of the current enlightened thinking about futures can be summarised in the following ten propositions, all of which can be explored in different ways in the classroom.

1.   The future is *not predictable*, neither is it predetermined.
2.   There thus exist a wide variety of *alternative futures*.
3.   These are commonly divided into *possible, probable and preferable* futures.
4.   Human decisions and actions/inactions *shape* the future.
5.   There is a need, therefore, for conscious *choice and participation* in relevant decision making.
6.   The present period is one of *unique importance* for future generations.
7.   It is necessary to *act responsibly* and on behalf of future generations when involved in change processes.
8.   Pre-action is always preferable to 'crisis learning'.
9.   *Holistic, global and long range* perspectives are all essential if we are to make sense of current trends.
10.   The *images* that we have of the future can act as powerful guides to actions in the present.

If we are really to educate young people for the 21st century, what sort of education do they need and how will the National Curriculum provide it? The new Global Futures Project was set up to specifically focus on the entitlement of young people to preparation for responsible and active citizenship as members of the global community.

The project arises out of, and will build on, much of the excellent work carried out in world studies during the last decade. It will help teachers and pupils look at four questions: Where are we now? How did we get here? Where do we want to go? And how will we get there? These questions can be applied both to our personal lives and to the world more generally.

Traditionally, subjects such as Science, Geography and History, and cross-curricular concerns such as world studies and environmental education have tended to focus on the first two of these questions. One result of this has often been to overwhelm young people with problems, in short to disempower them.

The Global Futures Project will focus, in particular, on the last two questions. It will help teachers' students to:

1.   *clarify* their choice of preferred futures at scales from the personal to the global;
2.   *envision* alternative futures which are both just and ecologically sustainable;
3.   *exercise* their rights responsibly in working for appropriate local and global change.

A central concern of the project will be identifying the nature of radical active citizenship in the local and global community. The project will also draw on utopian experiments from the past. In so doing it will honour a long-standing historical tradition of visionary commitment. Utopias are 'greenprints' for creating a better world. There is much to be learnt from them about the nature of the 'good life' and the 'good society' which is pertinent to the needs of the 21st century.

Over the next three years the project will work with teachers to produce appropriate resource materials for both primary and secondary pupils. It will be of interest to those concerned with foundation subjects such as Geography and English, Religious Education, and cross-curricular concerns such as personal and social education, environmental education and citizenship.

"A map without Utopia on it", wrote Robin Richardson, "is not worth consulting ... Admittedly there are disadvantages in dreams and ideals, the disadvantages of unreality and abstractions. But frequently it also clears and strengthens your mind if you venture to dream for a while, as concretely and as practically as possible, about the ideal situation to which all your current efforts are, you hope, directed". It is time now to do just that.

Reprinted from *Lib Ed*, Vol. 2 No. 13, Spring 1990.

Resources

The World Tomorrow, Chapter 7 of *World Studies 8-13: A Teacher's Handbook*, Fisher S and Hicks D, Oliver and Boyd, 1985.

The Temporal Dimension, Chapter 1 of *Global Teacher, Global Learner*, Pike G and Selby D, Hodder and Stoughton, 1988.

Futures, by Rick Slaughter, Chapter 13 in *Education for Peace: Issues, Principles and Practice in the Classroom*, ed. Hicks D, Routledge, 1989.

Understanding the World, Chapter 1 in *Making Global Connections: A World Studies Workbook*, eds. Hicks D and Steiner M, Oliver and Boyd, 1989.

The Sane Alternative: A Choice of Futures, Robertson J, 1983.

The Turning Point: Science, Society and the Rising Culture, Capra F, Flamingo/Fontana, 1983.

Teaching Resources for Education in International Understanding, Justice and Peace, published by the Marc Goldstein Memorial Trust, University of London Institute of Education, available from the Surrey Library of Teaching Resources, 6 Phoenice Cottages, Dorking Road, Bookham, Surrey, KT23 4QG (tel: 0372-56421), which has a mail order service.

... getting on with others ..., a resource pack on development education for youth work, produced by The Woodcraft Folk. Themes covered include: affirmation; cooperation; gender roles; anti-racism; links with other countries; the future.

Ten green battles

Technology is being given more and more emphasis on the timetables of British schoolchildren particularly through the 'new' subject of Craft, Design and Technology (CDT). But that doesn't have to mean more time spent marvelling at nuclear power stations and examining the innards of computers. With a bit of careful research and planning these classes can be turned into hotbeds of revolutionary activity. Here are some ideas...

CDT might seem one of the most staid departments in many schools, but surprisingly it can be the vehicle to introduce global, development and environmental issues into the curriculum. Courses can be developed which explicitly challenge racist and ethnocentric stereotypes, and which challenge the eurocentric view of the world. Sexism and bigoted views of disability can also be tackled.

1   The concepts of intermediate and appropriate technologies is a good starting point for older children. "An 'appropriate technology' is just that - appropriate to all the characteristics of the society. It may well also be an 'intermediate technology', one coming between a lower and a higher technological solution, but this may not necessarily be the case" explains one of the many useful publications from the education department of the Intermediate Technology Development Group (ITDG).

2   An excellent resource, published jointly by ITDG and the International Women's Tribune Centre, is the *Tech and Tools Book*. Its focus is technology appropriate to women.
How this book can be utilised in school is well illustrated by an ITDG education pack, *An appropriate stove for Sri Lanka*. In a non-patronising style it examines Sri Lanka's energy resources, the methods of cooking that are available to village families and the efforts of the Sarvodaya Shramadana Movement to improve the design of stoves.
The need for women's full involvement at all stages in the project, from design to installation, is emphasised, as is the inappropriateness of Western Technologies to the situation in Sri Lanka. Additional material looks at cooking stoves in Kenya, The Gambia and India.

3   ITDG, in their paper *Strategies and guidelines for teachers*, are careful to point out what teachers of development issues may be up against.
They list the teacher's own prejudices; the prejudices, racism and negative experiences of their pupils; our racial belief in the ethnic superiority of our society - both institutional and individual; and the negative stereotypes that people 'here' hold about people 'there'.
A project suggested by ITDG is the design of a delayed-release fishing float. Their leaflet, which unfortunately assumes that the fisher is always a man, sets the problem in the context of Third World fishing communities. However, their material is always careful to emphasise that Third World does not mean third rate and that many parallels can be drawn between situations faced by different groups of people *all* over the world.

4   Another 'off the shelf' worksheet available from ITDG is entitled *Design a blue cross veterinary box*. It describes the work of a village vet in Gujarat, India. The challenge offered is to design a box for the barefoot vets of India.

It must be: large enough to take all their equipment; light enough to be easily carried; sturdy enough to withstand transporting over country districts; able to offer some protection against sun and weather; easy to make from cheap local materials; and structured to prevent breakages.

Another similar project is offered by the Appropriate Health Resources and Technology Action Group. They publish *How to choose and make a cold box*.

5   The Centre for Alternative Technology (CAT), set up nearly twenty years ago, is another invaluable resource. They welcome visitors but as it is situated near Machynlleth, Powys, it may mean that a school trip there would only be possible as part of an expedition to the mountains of Wales.

Other similar but smaller projects can be found around Britain, and one of these may be well worth a school visit. The Urban Centre for Appropriate Technology in Bristol, for example.

CAT publishes a number of useful Do-It-Yourself plans which are invaluable for a technology classroom. One describes how you can make a 5 watt wind generator using a cycle wheel and hub dynamo. Another looks at solar power.

6   It has been estimated that were all aluminium cans recycled something like £13 million per year would be generated. Recycling is an ideal topic for a school project, for further information consult the Aluminium Re-cycling Can-paign or J Vogler's book *Work from Waste*, IT Publications.

7   A visit to the Horniman Museum and Library in Forest Hill, London, which contains the largest collection of tents in Britain would be an excellent starting point for a project investigating the design of living quarters for different environments.

8   Printing is an activity which many young people are fascinated by. A number of books are available from IT Publications which give practical instructions on AT processes: *Low cost printing for development* by Jonathan Zeitlyn; *The Low-cost Wooden Duplicator* by D Elcock; and *The Sten-screen: Making and using a low-cost printing process* by I McLaren.

9   A school itself is a great resource for many design and technology projects. How appropriate is the design of the classroom, the design of the dining hall or the library for people with disabilities. Does the building have wheelchair access? How could it be made more accessible?

10   Finally the revolutionary work of designers such as William Morris should not be forgotten. Plenty of material on Morris and his ideas is readily available.

Cliff Harper is a contemporary designer, some of whose utopian ideals might usefully be compared to those of William Morris.

Reprinted from *Lib Ed*, Vol.2 No. 12, Winter 1989.

Resources

Centre for Alternative Technology, Machynlleth, Powys, Wales.
Intermediate Technology Development Group, Rugby.
World Action for Recycling Materials and Energy from Rubbish (WARMER Campaign).
Chapter 12 of *Agenda for Multicultural Teaching*, Craft A and Klein G, SCDC/Longman, 1986.

Environmental Education

Everybody seems to want to be Green these days. But how can this revolution in thought be translated into the classroom? Here Ruth Coleman looks at Environmental Education - What it is, why it is necessary and how it can be achieved.

There have been many attempts to define the nature and scope of 'Environmental Education'. Perhaps this reflects its nature - it means different things to different people. Its scope is so wide that attempts to define it diminish its usefulness and potential. Schisms have developed in the movement, and only recently has the "act local, think global" ethos popularised by Friends of the Earth become a fully integrated part of the field. Traditionally the emphasis has been more on rural studies and, latterly, urban studies. "The study of the relationship between people and place" could then form a working definition.

The publication of *Environmental Education from 5- 16* (Curriculum Matters 13: an HMI series) made a welcome contribution to raising awareness about the role of Environmental Education in the school curriculum. The document provides a framework for consideration, but does not constitute a guarantee that Environmental Education will be firmly placed on the school agenda. It is, however, designated as one of five cross- curriculum themes within the National Curriculum.

This short booklet is certainly recommended reading for anybody interested in Environmental Education, and provides some useful ways forward for planning the school programme.

The past year has seen an unprecedented increase of interest in environmental issues. Concern for the well-being of the planet is reflected in everything, from the surge of support for green party politics in the European elections to the staggering increase in the membership of environmental organisations. If we really are to recycle up to 50% of all household waste by the year 2000, there will be a great demand for public information, education and action at all levels. The media, particularly childrens' television, have also played their part in informing and exposing various environmental wrong-doing.

On television in particular, the emphasis is on action - how you can contribute to wildlife conservation, how you can affect deforestation, how your efforts can raise money and protect the environment at the same time.

It seems to be the intention of the National Curriculum Council that the cross-curricular themes should be "included in attainment targets and programmes of study for the core and other foundation subjects". Exactly how Environmental Education, along with other cross-curricular themes (Economic Awareness, Personal and Social Education, Health Education, Careers Education) is to be delivered in terms of attainment targets is not made clear, though the relationship between most of these themes is clear.

Within a curriculum as congested as ours promises to be, it would seem to be more helpful to see Environmental Education as a theme-based approach through which attainment targets in core and foundation subjects can be delivered. Experience would suggest that if a programme of study is well planned it is then possible to "tick off" many of the attainment targets published so far. This approach is nothing new in many primary schools, but it can present problems in secondary education.

Following the publication of the Geography Working Group's Interim Report, we are likely to witness considerable negotiation between this subject area and science. The Report notes that "The statutory order for science contains one attainment target (AT5) 'Human Influences on the Earth' and another (AT9) entitled 'Earth and Atmosphere' ... impinges on geography ..." "The Secretaries of State should ask the National Curriculum Council and the Curriculum Council for Wales to recommend necessary changes to the science order which would remove from that order the content that is properly geographical, and would ensure a useful complementarity between the science and geographical curriculum".

We must hope that greater cooperation between these subject areas will become more widely evident to enable the breaking down of the rigid boundaries between subjects which are not always appropriate.

Another approach which secondary schools seem to be adopting is to hold an event or suspend the timetable for a day or two to explore environmental themes. Some have organised whole environmental weeks, others have planned to put two days aside to look at an issue and develop it into a programme of study. One Avon school actually uses such activities to bridge the gap between leaving their fifth year and joining the sixth form.

A common problem in planning a programme of Environmental Education is the tendency to take on too much. A focus on a specific environmental issue will usually lead to others. It is important to restrict the field of study as one runs the danger of over-simplifying the issues, and not developing an integrated view of the complexities inherent in the relationship between environmental issues. This will be further influenced by the National Curriculum in future. For example, science advisory teachers have commented on the lack of resources available for infant science as it appears in the statutory orders. Attainment target 1 (Exploration of Science) levels 1-2, Attainment target 5 (Human Influences on the Earth) up to level 4 and levels 1-3 of Attainment target 6 (Types and uses of materials) could be achieved through simple recycling experiments in which the number of items both organic and inorganic could be buried and checked over a period of time.

As pupils become older, an issue-based approach seems to work best. Whether this is looking at a local planning issue - for example deciding where the best place for a zebra crossing may be, looking at uses for a piece of derelict ground, or even how the school grounds could be improved - seems to be the most helpful. A teachers pack on green consumerism currently being prepared by Bristol Friends of the Earth illustrates the cross- curricular nature of Environmental Education very well, and also embraces the "think local, act global" ethos.

The pack has developed as the result of a survey to expose many of the false claims made by supermarket chains as they compete to open up new markets by launching 'green' products. The pack will offer worksheets to be used by pupils on topics such as Food, Packaging, Cleaning materials, Paper products and About the Shop.

Each worksheet will include survey work to be conducted by pupils as a fieldwork exercise. This part of the pack will concentrate on the skills of observation and recording. Several schools who have used the survey set these tasks as homework, particularly if there were practical problems of using school time. Pupils are provided with a glossary of terms that are either used in the questions or are likely to be found in the shop or on the products under scrutiny.

Classroom follow-up work will develop skills of analysis and evaluation, and encourage a fuller understanding of the issues involved. Many of the questions and findings are formulated to prompt further investigation into, for example, trade links with developing countries, particularly through cost comparison; who might buy the most over-packaged product in the store and why; implications for energy consumption, comparing transport options available to get to the store; and the relationship between food additives and health.

Clearly there is ample opportunity for the study of the core, foundation and cross-curricular themes in this pack.

At secondary level it is important to undertake some political education. Pupils (and a vast number of adults) know little about how environmental decisions are made. This is vital foundation work if a balanced understanding of environmental concerns is to be gained. How else can individuals become empowered to influence action and change within the environment?

A further useful tool, particularly in this area of environmental decision-making, is the use of role-play, and of simulation exercises. Role-play is particularly useful in coming to an understanding of the conflicting pressures on land use. It also contributes to more sophisticated thinking. Simulation exercises of, for example, local government committee practice or land development games, are fun, ice-breaking, and generally absorb the full attention of the participants. It is possible to use some of these techniques in a workshop. It is, however, important to develop a full programme of work rather than a series of unrelated activities.

The most crucial factor in successful Environmental Education in schools is making sure that the study begins from where the children are. It is vital to start from their own experience, increasing environmental awareness as a first stage and then building on this. Neither is there any substitute for direct experience of as many environments as possible. Schools are frequently asking for more information for school projects on, for example, what local people think about public transport provision. The answer is always the same - go out and ask them! We can only hope that schools will not be deterred from conducting educationally valuable field trips, since the rules regarding charging for school visits have changed, and safety in outdoor education has become an issue for concern.

Reprinted from *Lib Ed*, Vol 2. No. 14, Summer 1990.

Resources

GCSE Coursework Enquiry Guide - Geography, Network Educational Press, PO Box 635, Rode, Bath, BA3 3FB (tel: 0373-830833).

Science for Survival - Plants and Rainforests in the Classroom, Adam Cade, Richmond Publishing, WWF-UK Environmental Education Project.

The Design and Planning Games Pack, Jeff Bishop and Graham Russell, Resources for Learning Development Unit, Bishop Road, Bishopston, Bristol, BS7 8LS (tel: 0272-428208).

Local Issues - Geography Matters, Robert Stephenson, Nelson.

Inside Outside - An Action Plan for Improving the Primary School Environment, Robert Stephenson and Cherry Mares, Tidy Britain Group, The Pier, Wigan, WN3 4EX.

Curriculum Matters 13: Environmental Education from 5-16, HMSO.

Nature Areas and the Primary School Curriculum, The Nature Conservancy Council, Publications Dept., Northminster House, Peterborough, PE1 1UA (tel: 0733-40345 x2211). They also produce a number of colourful and informative wallcharts, posters, slide/tape packs and books.

Watch Leaders Activity Pack, 22 The Green, Nettleham, Lincs., LN2 2NR (tel: 0522-752326).

Making Playgrounds, a set of posters, books, worksheets and slides about planning, designing and building interesting and imaginative playgrounds, Community Service Volunteers, 237 Pentonville Road, London, N1 9NJ (tel: 071-278-6601).

The Council for Environmental Education produces and extensive list of resources and review teaching materials in a regular newssheet, Faculty of Education and Community Studies, University of Reading, London Road, Reading, RG1 5AQ (tel: 0734-318921).

Sharing Nature with Children, Joseph Bharret Cornall, Exley Press.

Dead musicians society

Music has the potential to allow students to develop their ability to express themselves, yet all too often ends up as another trial of rote learning. Here David Gribble, of Sands School, discusses the potential of music teaching, and where it goes horribly wrong.

Music is an opportunity for self-expression. It is therefore strange that almost all instrumental teaching is directed at enabling people to express only what someone else has written. It is as if music were limited to the art of imitating other musicians. A hundred years ago art students used to copy famous paintings. Piano students are still copying famous music.

I had my first piano lessons fifty years ago. First you had to struggle to play sequences of notes that had been specially written for beginners and had very little interest in themselves as tunes.

Then you went on to pieces which sounded pretty good when the teacher played them, but which took you several weeks to learn to play through, even slowly, with frequent mistakes and no expression. When you progressed as far as expression, you found that that too had all been written for you, mostly, for some extraordinary reason, in Italian.

For a long time I seriously believed that it was impossible to play music unless it had been previously written down.

In terms of language, this would mean that it was possible to read out loud, but not to speak spontaneously. Trying to play by ear, or worse still, to extemporise, was just mucking about. When I learnt that traditional jazz bands played without any music at all, I thought it must be the result of some kind of telepathy.

Now I play jazz quite a lot, at a fairly simple level, and in doing so I depend far too much on my knowledge of basic chords, and I am still far too often unable to play what I hear in my head because I am afraid I'll get it wrong as I haven't seen it written down. Although I can recognise written notes, without an instrument I can only work out very simple tunes indeed, and even then I'm not sure I'm right. I had piano lessons for most of my school years, on and off, and in the succeeding forty years I have still not overcome a number of basic blocks.

Is there a way of teaching music which would have avoided my unhappy and unsuccessful hours with the Moonlight Sonata on the one hand, and on the other developed what musical talents I have so that I could play by ear, and read and write straightforward tunes without having to try them out on an instrument first?

I put this question to Julian Marshall, graduate of the Royal College of Music, half of the 70s pop-group Marshall Hain, jazz musician and currently, among other things, teacher of composition at Dartington College of Arts, piano teacher at Sands School and parent at Park School, where his parental contribution of three hours a week takes the form of music workshops.

His first response was to say that my reaction to the teaching I had had was almost universal among the adults who came to him for lessons, and his second response was to say that this problem with music pin-pointed the question of how much education is about the amassing of knowledge, and how much it is about helping children to learn to explore for themselves.

He illustrated his ideas by describing the activities he uses in his occasional music workshops. He covers a variety of topics in any one workshop, but none of them depend on any previously acquired musical knowledge.

He tries to help the participants experience and respond to some of the elements of music, for instance he may start with rhythm games. Groups may be asked to pass a clap round a circle, first straightforwardly and then backwards, backwards and forwards simultaneously, missing out every other person and so on or they may play the game of copy-cats or perform rhythm rounds.

Sometimes he divides people into small groups to make rhythm machines, when they use not merely their hands for clapping but also their voices, feet and any other part of the body. This last exercise helps people to understand that you don't need an instrument to make music - you are the instrument yourself, and if you use a piano or a trumpet to help you, you are only using it as a machine.

Another activity involves making people aware of the sounds that surround us all the time. He may invite children to think of all the noises that you might hear in the kitchen, and then tell a story purely in sounds. Another more complex version is to invite them to improvise the sound-track of a film with dialogue, sound-effects and music.

An orchestra with a conductor but no instruments, in which different groups produce different sounds or rhythms in response to the conductor's gestures indicating stop, start, louder and softer, is immense fun and can produce extraordinarily interesting effects. Again this illustrates that music does not come out of instruments, it comes out of people.

Listening to music is also likely to be a part of a workshop. Julian will play five or six fairly short contrasting pieces, asking the listeners not to judge them, not to decide whether they like them or not, but just to let them in anyway, and then to write or draw images associated with the music. Even rowdy groups of eight-year-olds have listened for as long as thirty minutes, with spectacular responses, and adults have been at it for two hours at a time.

The important thing about this approach is that it demonstrates that what matters is the intention and involvement of the performer. Technical perfection is an irrelevance, and indeed technically perfect machines are taking all the feeling out of pop music.

Society as a whole seems to believe that the more complex something is the better it is, and student musicians apply this to music. This is quite inappropriate; an example is the way inexperienced jazz musicians feel they have to fill every second of their solos with notes, whereas the great performers have time to listen and wait.

How, I wanted to know, does this kind of approach lead to the actual learning of how to play an instrument? Again, the important thing is the intention of the student.

Students must have some idea of how they want to use the instrument for themselves. Their learning then becomes purposeful in quite a different way from that of the student who only wants to know how to work out what the notes mean.

The most valuable lesson Julian learnt in all his musical education was from a teacher at the Royal College of Music; when Julian asked him about a technical difficulty in a piece, this teacher gave him no technical advice, but instead helped him to see the passage in context as a part of the musical whole; the technical difficulty would then resolve itself.

Most children asking for piano lessons ask because they want to pass grades, or learn to play particular pieces. They do not want to use the piano for the exploration of sound, and are often not interested by being asked to use the instrument to create expressive sounds.

They want to be imitative, they want to learn pieces by rote, because that is what other people do, that is what music seems to them to be. It is as if the left side of the brain were trying to take over what only has meaning as a right brain activity.

Julian feels that children have to go on the route they themselves have chosen, but he also wants to push them to try to do things they might otherwise feel they were not able to do.

There is little pleasure in listening to music played accurately but without feeling, whereas the emotional involvement of a musician can be inspiring even without much technique. Obviously it is an advantage for a musician to be able to pick up a piece of music and play it, but it is much better first to be able to create music of your own.

I returned to my own problems, and gave as an illustration the fact that I still cannot play the simple Haydn pieces I was first given to learn when I was about twelve. He told me that I was looking at it purely as an intellectual exercise, an interpretation of written symbols. If I really wanted to learn to play Haydn, then I should start by listening to a lot of Haydn.

Of course I know that you can't play jazz until you have heard it. Why had I never thought of Haydn in the same way?

Reprinted from *Lib Ed*, Vol. 2 No. 16, Summer 1991.

New Games for old

One of the *Lib ED* Collective discusses co-operative games, their development and their relevance to education today.

New Games aren't necessarily new - what is different about them is the style. Many of us have been playing New Games for quite a while, perhaps without realising it. So what are they?

Firstly a bit of history. New Games originated in the USA in the early 70s. Influenced by the Vietnam war, Stewart Brand came up with the idea of working out aggression in a 'safe' environment, and invented the wonderfully named "Slaughter". 'Softwar' games caught on and, in conjunction with Pat Farrington, New Games developed to include trust and non-competitive games. The success of the first New Games Tournament ensured their spread across the USA and the world. New Games UK is an organisation with the aim of promoting these games through information, equipment and training workshops.

I'm not going to go into great detail about the theory behind New Games here - for that you can contact New Games UK, or work it out yourselves by playing them. The difference between these games and traditional ones is the style. Most traditional games are based on competition, exclusion and division; New Games are about co-operation, inclusion and unity. Let me explain.

Firstly, they are about encouraging everybody to participate. This is done by devising games which allow everybody to join in without the danger of being made to feel inferior, unsafe, merely tolerated or just plain stupid, and putting no pressure on people to participate. New Games can be played by the young, old, disabled, able-bodied, female, male, everybody - all at once if that is what the group consists of. This is the epitome of inclusion.

Secondly, New Games break down the barriers of race, class, hierarchy and sex. They can help us to be more relaxed with one another. Many games break down our fear of touch and help us to realise that touch isn't necessarily sexual. They can also provide us with that feeling of being needed without stressful demands being made. All of this is very therapeutic.

They also provide a necessary compliment (antidote) to the usual competitive games that we all know and love (hate). Too much stress is laid upon competition in our society. Many essentially non-competitive activities are made competitive, for instance geography in schools.

I am not against competition - indeed some New Games are competitive - but it is the over-emphasis that is harmful. To have winners you must have losers "no matter how many socks they pull up, belts they pull in or bicycles they get on." (John Butler) New Games prove that we can have fun without competing. "There is nothing wrong with competition in the proper proportion. Like salt it adds zest to the game and to life itself. But when seasoning is mistaken for the substance, only sickness can follow." (George Leonard)

Finally, New Games are about having fun. The philosphy goes as follows - these games are fun, are not based on superiority/inferiority, embarassment, exclusion, and so on, and so if you are not having fun it is your responsibility. They are about re-capturing (holding on to?) the spirit of playfulness that we all had when we were children, about dropping our defences and playing for no other reason than enjoyment.

New Games are about people. While there are basic games that can be played, these can be modified by players to suit the needs of the group - in fact modifications are positively encouraged. We can bend the rules - which are kept to a minimum anyway - and so put people first. Cheating is out of the question, as diversions from the rules tend to become the new rules. Certainly I have yet to hear somebody complain about cheating.

It's all about equality. Everybody that takes part is equal, especially as no importance is attached to winning. Referees become co-players, players become referees. The only difference initially is experience, confidence and willingness to take a risk. Once the game is going referees become virtually redundant.

If you are interested, why not contact New Games UK, PO Box 542, London, NW2 3PQ, or me, Clive, through the *Libertarian Education* contact address.

Resources

Games, Games, Games, A Cooperative Games Book produced by The Woodcraft Folk (200 games).

Parachutes and play canopies - You may be able to get an 'expired' parachute from a parachute club, or even the RAF!

The Lanmoor Activity Canopy, produced by Nottingham Handicrafts Ltd., 17 Ludlow Hill road, Melton Road, West Bridgeford, Nottingham (tel: 0602-234251).

Parachute Canopies, produced by Hestair Hope educational Suppliers, Hestair Hope Ltd., St Philips Drive, Royton, Oldham, OL2 6AG (tel: 061-652-1411).

Play Canopies, produced by Gasworks Childrens Play Equipment, Hull Innovation Centre, Guildford Road, Queens Gardens, Hull, HV1 1HJ (tel: 0482-226348).

Games

BALL OFF - All but a few players hold the parachute, the others go underneath and try to push a ball placed on top off. Players at the edge can use a hand to keep it on.

CHANGEOVER - Players 'mushroom' (see below) the parachute, and then some run under it. The leader can call who these are to be, for example those with blue socks.

THE DICE GAME - Players form a circle. One player goes to stand in front of another, and this pair follow these actions: Cup hands as if holding a dice, shake three times while counting one, two, three ... then together they choose and either raise hands to shoulder height and say "Hello", or they lower hands to below waist height and say "No". If they both choose the same action, they both set off to find another partner to play with. If they choose different actions, then the player in the circle stays there until they are given another chance.

DOMINOES - Players form a long single file line. The front player falls back into the arms of the second player who must catch them and lower them to the ground before starting their turn. They do the same thing so as to give the 'domino' effect to the line. As the 4th or 5th person falls the front person stands up and runs to join the back, and so on. How long can it keep going?

DRAGON DODGEBALL - Players form a circle enclosing a number of short 'dragons' (2 or 3 people in a line). The players in the circle throw soft balls to hit the dragons bottom. A successful thrower joins the back of the dragon hit and sends the front of that particular dragon back into the circle.

INFINITY VOLLEYBALL - All the players try to keep a large beach ball up in the air. Count how many times you can hit it.

KNOTS - Players stand shoulder to shoulder in a small circle and, with eyes closed, reach into the centre to take hold of two other peoples hands. They then open their eyes and without breaking hands have to 'untangle' themselevs.

LEAF IN THE WIND - In small groups, one player lays on the floor and is gently lifted by the others of the group and swayed from side to side.

LOOSE CABOOSE - Players stand in pairs, one behind the other , in a circle. There is one loose caboose who runs from a person who is 'it'. If the loose caboose needs a rest, they stand at the front of one of the other pairs, becoming the front person. The one at the back lets go and becomes the new 'loose caboose'.

MUSHROOM - Players hold the parachute near to the ground and, on the command of 'mushroom', lift the parachute above their heads.

MUSICAL CHAIRS - Exactly as the tradtional version, except that people who can't find a chair to sit on should be offered a lap by some kind player who does have one. The game should end with everybody sitting on one chair!

OCTOPUS - Players begin at one edge of the play space, and an 'octopus' stands in the centre. The fishes at the edge have to 'swim' across the play space to the other side without being touched by the 'octopus'. If they are, then they become a stationary 'tentacle' of the 'octopus', and may also 'have' other fish swimming past.

RAINDROPS - Players stand in a circle with right shoulders towards the centre. Basically you do to the person in front whatever happens to you. The leader starts by tapping finger tips on the nape of the neck, then runs fingers down back, rubs shoulder blades, gently 'thumps' shoulder blades, pushes forward a few small steps and then repeats these in reverse!

RAINSTORM - In a circle the leader makes sounds which are passed or copied by each player round the circle. For best effect silence and eyes closed can be requested. One sequence of actions might be, rubbing hands together, clapping 2 fingers onto your palm, clicking fingers, slapping thighs, stamping feet and then these in reverse.

SAY GOODBYE - Your dearest friend is going away and you've come to see them off. The farewell can be as affectionate as you want. Hugs, tears and kisses are all in order.

SLAP TAG - Two teams stand either side of the playing area facing each other. Players hold hands in front of them. A raider from one team goes to the other and slaps one of the outstretched hands. When touched the player chases the raider who tries to escape back to their own team. If caught, the raider swops sides, if not, the raider keeps the 'pursuer'.

SLAUGHTER - There are two teams, one without shoes and one without shoes or socks. There are two goals and two balls. The players must be on their knees to prevent the game getting out of hand. The idea is to score by getting the ball into your opponents goal. Almost anything goes. If you are forced out of the playing area, then you either drop out or you join the other side. The game stops when everybody is exhausted.

WINK MURDER - All the players close their eyes whilst the leader chooses some 'murderers' by tapping them on the shoulder. The players then 'mingle' with eyes open. The murderers 'kill' by winking at people. These then 'die' as dramatically as is possible. If a player who is not killed suspects another player of being a 'killer', they stop and shout "I accuse", at which all players stop and listen to the accusation. If the accusation is correct, the 'killer' is 'killed', if not then it is the accuser who is killed.

Liberation for people with disabilities

It is undeniable that during this century there have been a series of inspiring, if sometimes short lived, projects designed to liberate children from the shackles of coercive and unpleasant schooling. However, the many questions that surround the complex questions of how to tackle the liberation of learning for people with disabilities seems to have scarcely been touched.

The reasons for this are many. People with disabilities often have little in common with each other, except for the fact that society disables them.

It seems much healthier to look at the situation of people with disabilities as being people for whom society has to make adaptations, rather than being people who have to adapt to society.

Despite the suggestion that the categorisation of people with disabilities turns them into merely medical cases, and can obscure their real, human and individual needs, it seems realistic to suggest that there are people who have a range of physical, sensory and learning difficulties. It is also realistic that society should make major adaptations to its physical structures (for example access to buildings), attitudes ("they can't ... because they're handicapped") and activities in order to give people with disabilities a chance to participate fully on their own terms.

Media representations of disability are often treacherous, most books are manuals of helpful things to do, some organisations seem to be run on a paternalistic basis. For example the Royal National Institute for the Blind translated the text of Chaucer's Miller's Tale into braille for a girl who was doing A level English with all the naughty bits removed! But here, hopefully, are some positive suggestions.

Media

Does he take sugar? Radio 4

Books

Including Pupils with Disabilities, edited by Tony Booth and Will Swann. Open University Press.

The Nature of Special Education, edited by Tony Booth and June Statham. Open University Press.

There are a number of books around now which deal with the integration of children with special needs into ordinary schools. In spite of the many reservations that one may feel about ordinary schools, it has to be remembered that for many children this represents the first step out of the ghetto.

Organisations

There are an increasing number of parental self-support groups in different parts of the country. There are also an increasing number of groups run by, or for, people with disabilities. The only way to find out how useful these are is to attend them.

Nationally there is the *Liberation Network for People with Disabilities*, c/o Townsend House, Green Lanes, Marshfield, Chippenham, Wiltshire.

Schools

Generally there has been some progress in the nature of Special Education over the last ten years. It is true that professionals are starting to question what they do, and the assumptions behind their practices much more closely. There have been attempts to make the system more client-centred, rather than disability-centred.

The Steiner Foundation run a number of Special Schools (called Camphill Schools) and, as yet *Lib ED* has not visited them. It is understood that they are pleasant, but may suffer from the problem of ghettoisation, one of the main problems for special schools.

There has been an attempt to integrate children with most disabilities into ordinary schools, even on a minimal basis- this can only have a beneficial effect on mainstream schoolchildren (and teachers) many of whom are as ignorant as the rest of the population even of the existence of their peers who have major problems. Unfortunately the combination of the demands of the National Curriculum and Local Financial Management will discourage these partial integration schemes. Much needs to be done in this area ...

Education Otherwise

Modern industrial societies are obsessed with schooling. Children are processed en masse into standardised products of the education machine. Yet resistant forms emerge. Critics of these factory methods spring up and refuse to submit their offspring for processing... Over more than ten years these 'deviants' have become increasingly well organised and advertising themselves as Education Otherwise now claim a membership of almost two thousand.

Education Otherwise was set up in 1977 to help provide an alternative to the cruelty and conformity of state schooling. Practising principles of mutual aid, decentralised organisation and tolerance, it has grown enormously, yet retained its openness. The emphasis has always been on helping each other, rather than on establishing a strict "party line"

Although members share a common mistrust of schooling, they don't always agree on what constitutes good educational practice. While most want to offer children more freedom and choice, some embark on home education in order to retain more control over their children and their curriculum. Yet, faced with a predatory state system always on the lookout for more child victims, differences have been contained and members have co-operated in establishing their right to educate otherwise ...

It shall be the duty of the parent of every child of compulsory school age to cause him to receive efficient full-time education suitable to his age, ability and aptitude and to any special educational needs he may have either by regular attendance at school or otherwise
1944 Education Act: Section 36

EO points out to parents that the law recognises that they have primary reponsibility for their children's education, and whilst they may delegate this to schools they need not do so. They may choose to "educate otherwise". If they don't register their children at a school in the first place they should have no problem with the education authorities. If a parent wants to withdraw a child from a state school at which they have been registered it's a bit more complicated.

They have to convince the LEA that the child, once de-registered, will still receive an efficient, appropriate education. In practice it's usually an "educational advisor" from the LEA who needs convincing, and EO helps members to do this effectively. Most LEAs then accept the home education with only an occasional enquiry about curriculum or timetable, some are even prepared to lend books and equipment.

A few take a more aggressive line, and EO is called upon to help defend parents from legal threats and court action. Sometimes authorities are even more vindictive, and on occasions have threatened to take EO kids into care, but the combination of legal expertise and collective support has generally succeeded in keeping EO children out of the clutches of the state system.

EO is open to anybody who supports the idea of home education, whether they're a practitioner or not. Membership costs around ten pounds per year, but they'll negotiate if you can't afford it. The members are scattered throughout Britain, with a few people overseas. To maintain local contacts there's a system of seventy or so regional coordinators, who organise local meetings and events, and generally keep members in the area in touch with each other.

The effectiveness of these coordinators varies a lot from region to region, so the main means of communication in EO is undoubtedly provided by the bi-monthly newsletter. This well-produced forty-page booklet carries not only nitty gritty details of meetings, information and letters, but original, provocative articles that raise many important issues about education and children's rights.

Recognising the key role of the newsletter, which is open to all interested members, EO revolves the editorship with each issue. Those functions which are more centralised, such as the finances, are at least separated geographically; the membership secretary might be in Rosshire, the Treasurer in Chester, the PR Officer in Surrey, and so on.

EO's commitment to decentralism is further shown by the publication and distribution of a comprehensive contact list to each member, together with the details of any skills offered. This allows and encourages members to contact each other directly without going through any hierarchy or committee.

Children's right to decide on their own education is enshrined in EO's statement of aims and objectives, though it is not recognised as absolute, as we have seen. At EO get-togethers it is clear that adult/child relationships are generally enlightened with children given as much freedom and respect as adults, though some parents do choose the otherwise option in order to gain maximum control of their children's lives.

The more obvious examples are the EO parents who claim schools are no longer academic enough, or too concerned with sex education, but there are more subtle authoritarians. Some of the cases of school phobia, for example, are more to do with the insecurity, possessiveness and neuroses of the parents than the undoubted cruelty of the school system. For children trapped in such unloving, repressive homes there's no otherwise option ...

Let's get off children's backs and let them learn what they want, when they want. Learning grows where it will, where the soil and climate are right. We can no more ordain learning by order, coercion and commandment than we can produce love by rape or threat **Peter Jones** EO Newsletter 34

Having made the great leap of removing their kids from the over-structured world of school, parents sometimes lose their courage. Peter Jones' diatribe was directed against the tendency amongst some EO parents to slip back into a system of lessons, tests and formal teaching that they set out to avoid. Ironically it's often those parents who have had most formal education themselves who feel most confident about letting go of their children's learning.

Recognising the problems of the less confident parent, EO has published a booklet *Early Years*, which shows how you can support your child's learning without directing it. The philosophy is "learning without teaching", which is greatly assisted by the environment of EO. Where the most progressive schools try to teach through problem solving and simulation exercises, the EO child is learning by solving real problems, by living the reality that schools seek to simulate.

Education Otherwise is clearly a success, yet one which has its limitations. The first concerns EOs commitment to children's rights. EO may officially recognise children's autonomy, but what about the minority of members who don't practice this principle? EO should withdraw help and refuse membership to parents who seem to be taking children out of school for their own benefit rather than that of the child.

This might be a difficult policy to operate, but it is necessary if EO is to be clearly identified as part of kids lib rather than just parents lib. The appointment of a co-ordinator responsible for monitoring and supporting the role of children within the organisation would also strengthen this approach.

The middle class domination of EO is also a concern. There are some working class members, but it is clearly much easier to educate otherwise if the family income is high enough to support an adult staying at home full-time. Much of EOs press publicity tends to appear in places more apparent to the middle class, like the Observer, Country Life and Radio Four.

EO is aware of this limitation, but has no strategy to remedy it. In fact their overall strategy might itself be seen as middle class: to avoid confrontation and work within the system, to pursue individual cases but not to generalise campaigns. This allows for maximum practical progress but limits political change.

Despite these limitations, during its ten year history EO has enabled many kids to escape humiliation and failure, and gain self-confidence and happiness. From nothing it has created a valuable alternative to the state schooling system. It has achieved this within a libertarian organisational framework, an expanding membership and a sound financial base. It is an important achievement in the long struggle for the liberation of learning.

Reprinted from *Lib ED*, Vol. 2 No. 5, Summer 1987

A prominent member of EO responded to this article with the following letter, which was published in *Lib ED* Vol. 2 No. 7, Spring 1988.

In your last issue you suggested that Education Otherwise should withdraw help and refuse membership to parents who take their children out of school for their own benefit rather than that of the child; and further "the appointment of a co-ordinator responsible for monitoring and supporting the role of children within the organisation".

You are suggesting that EO becomes an authority able to decide who should and should not be members! Surely, we don't need an alternative authority. The suggestion is strictly in opposition to liberation.

The freedom to choose an appropriate form of education is not in doubt. (Education is compulsory though school is not). If you start qualifying the use of this freedom that questioning may undermine the right to educate at home. It will cause undue upset and probably divide EO as a movement. It may also create a mafioso of watch-dogs, ready to pounce on "parents-rights operators". It may well destroy EO.

Leave well alone. EO has achieved much, against opposition. Its steady increase over the last eleven years both in its membership and its own awareness, its capacity for consciousness raising without pushing its beliefs too hard, make it a truly organic movement, giving support and practical help to parents and children who wish to choose educational options other than school. Any abuse of its integral beliefs by individual members is far outweighed by EO's positively liberating principles. That is, the liberation of both child and parent and the necessary mutual respect that such liberation implies.

Poppy Green

See also the Children's Home-Based Education Association, address in the directory.

Bibliography

Rather than take subjective and contentious decisions about whether this or that writer is 'libertarian', we include a range of books which we believe will be of special interest to libertarian educationalists.

Books

Ackerman, Nathan W. and others, *Summerhill: For and Against* (New York: Hart 1970)

Adams, Sir John, *Modern Developments in Educational Practice* (2nd edn: University of London Press 1928)

Adams, Leonard D. (ed), *Francisco Ferrer, His Life, Work and Martyrdom* (New York: Francisco Ferrer Association 1910)

Adams, Paul and others, *Children's Rights* (Elek Books 1971)

Adelstein, David, *The Wisdom and Wit of R.S.Peters* (University of London Institute of Education Students' Union 1971)

ALTARF, *Challenging Racism* (ALTARF 1984)

Antistudent Pamphlet Collective, *Antistudent* (1972)

Armistead, Nigel and others, *Rat, Myth and Magic* (1972)

Armstrong, Michael, *Closely Observed Children* (Writers and Readers 1980)

Armytage, W.H.G., *Heavens Below: Utopian Experiments in England 1560-1960* (RKP 1961)

Ash, Maurice, *Who Are The Progressives Now?* (RKP 1969)

Ashton-Warner, Sylvia, *Teacher* (Penguin 1970)

Avrich, Paul, *The Modern School Movement: Anarchism and Education in the United States* (New Jersey: Princeton University Press 1980)

Badley, J.H., *Bedales: A Pioneer School* (1923)

Baker, Joy, *Children in Chancery* (Hutchinson 1964)

Bakunin, Mikhail, *Integral Education* (Cambridge, Mass.: Cambridge Free Press 1986)

Ball, Colin and Ball, Mog, *Education for a Change* (Penguin 1973)

Barbiana, School of, *Letter to a Teacher* (Penguin 1970; first published in Italy 1969)

Barrowfield Community School, *Progress Report* (Aberdeen Peoples Press 1975)

Bauer, W.W., *Stop Annoying Your Children* (New York: Bobbs-Merrill 1947)

Bazely, E.T., *Homer Lane and the Little Commonwealth* (Allen and Unwin 1928)

Beacock, D.A., *Play Way: English for Today: The Methods and Influence of Caldwell Cook* (Nelson 1943)

Berg, Leila, *Look at Kids* (Penguin 1972)

Berg, Leila, *Reading and Loving* (RKP 1977)

Berg, Leila, *Risinghill: Death of a Comprehensive School* (Penguin 1968)

Berg, Leila, see Walmsley, John

Blewitt, Trevor (ed), *The Modern Schools Handbook* (Gollancz 1934)

Blishen, Edward (ed), *The School That I'd Like* (Penguin 1969)

Bonham-Carter, Victor, *Dartington Hall: The Formative Years 1925-1956* (Phoenix House 1958)

Bookchin, Murray, *Post Scarcity Anarchism* (Wildwood House 1974)

Bowles, Samuel and Gintis, Herbert, *Schooling in Capitalist America* (Routledge and Kegan Paul 1976)

Boyd, W., *Towards a New Education* (A.A.Knopf 1930)

Boyd, W. and Rawson, W., *The Story of the New Education* (Heinemann 1965)

Brand, N., *Early Days in the Forest School*

Brantingham, Tony, *In Place of School* (1973)

Bridgeland, M. *Pioneer Work with Maladjusted Children* (StaplesPress 1971)

Brinton, Maurice, *Authoritarian Conditioning, Sexual Repression and the Irrational in Politics* (Solidarity 1974)

Buckman, Peter (ed) *Education Without Schools* (Souvenir Press 1973)

Burn, Michael, *Mr. Lyward's Answer* (Hamish Hamilton 1956)

Campaign for State Supported Alternative Schools, *A Case for Alternative Schools Within the Maintained System* (Advisory Centre for Education 1980)

Campaign to Impede Sex Stereotyping in the Young, *CISSY Talks to Publishers* (1974)

Carnoy, Martin, *Education as Cultural Imperialism* (New York: McKay 1964)

Castles, S. and Wustenburg, W. *The Education of the Future* (Pluto Press 1979)

Centre for Contemporary Cultural Studies, *Unpopular Education* (Hutchinson 1981)

Chanan, Gabriel and Gilchrist, Linda, *What School is For* (Methuen 1974)

Child, H.A.T. (ed), *The Independent Progressive School* (Hutchinson 1962)

Chilton Pearce,J. Magical Child (Granada 1979)

Clarke, Sir Fred, *Freedom in the Educative Society* (University of London Press 1948)

Clegg, Alec (ed), *The Changing Primary School* (Chatto and Windus 1972)

Clemencau, G. *La Melee Sociale* (Paris: Charpetier et Fusquelle 1895)

Coard, Bernard, *How the West Indian Child is Made Educationally Subnormal in the British School System* (New Beacon Books 1971)

Cohen, P. and Bains, H.S. (eds) *Multi-racist Britain* (Macmillan 1988)

Cook, H. Caldwell, *The Play Way* (Heinemann 1917)

Cornforth, Maurice, *Rebels and Their Causes: Essays in Honour of A.L.Morton* (Lawrence and Wishart 1978)

Craik, William W., *The Central Labour College* (Lawrence and Wishart 1964)

Croall, Jonathan, *Neill of Summerhill: The Permanent Rebel* (RKP 1983)

Croall, Jonathan (ed), *All the Best, Neill: Letters from Summerhill* (Andre Deutsch 1983)

Croft, Michael, *Spare the Rod* (Longman 1954)

Cudihy, Bob, Gown, Douglas and Lindsay, Colin, *The Red Paper* (Edinburgh: Islander Publications 1970)

Curry, W.B., *Education for Sanity* (1947)

Curry, W.B. *The School* (John Lane 1934)

Deakin, M., *The Children on the Hill* (Quartet 1973)

Deem, Rosemary, *Women and Schooling* (RKP 1978)

Dennison, George, *The Lives of Children* (Penguin 1972; first published in USA 1969)

Dewey, John, *Art as Experience* [1934] (New York: Capricorn Books 1958)

Dewey, John, *The Child and the Curriculum* [1902] and *The School and Society* [1899] (Chicago: University of Chicago Press 1963)

Dewey, John, *Democracy and Education* (New York: Macmillan 1916)

Dewey, John, *Experience and Education* [1938] (New York: Collier 1963)

Dewey, John and Dewey, Evelyn, *Schools of Tommorrow* [1915] (NewYork: Dutton 1962)

Dixon, Bob, *Catching Them Young 1: Sex, Race and Class in Children's Fiction* (Pluto Press 1977)

Dixon, Bob, *Catching Them Young 2: Political Ideas in Children's Fiction* (Pluto Press 1977)

Dolgoff, Sam (ed), *Bakunin on Anarchy* (1972)

Dummett, A., *A Portrait of English Racism* (CARAF 1984)

Edwards, Bertram, *The Burston School Strike* (Lawrence and Wishart 1974)

Edwards, Stewart (ed), *Selected Writings of Pierre-Joseph Proudhon* (New York: Garden City 1969)

Ellis, Terry and others, *William Tyndale: The Teachers' Story* (Writers and Readers 1976)

Elmhirst, L.V., *Rabindranath Tagore: Pioneer in Education* (Murray 1961)

Ferrer, Francisco, *The Origins and Ideals of the Modern School* (Watts 1913)

Fishman, William J., *East End Jewish Radicals 1875-1914* (Duckworth 1975)

Fletcher, Colin, Caron, Maxine and Williams, Wyn, *Schools on Trial* (Open University Press 1985)

Franklin, Bob (ed), *The Rights of Children* (Basil Blackwell 1986)

Freeman, Jo and Levine, Cathy, *Untying the Knot (Feminism, Anarchism and Organisation)* (Dark Star/Rebel Press 1984)

Freire, Paulo, *Cultural Action for Freedom* (Penguin 1972; first published in USA 1970)

Freire, Paulo, *Education for Critical Consciousness* (Sheed and Ward 1974)

Freire, Paulo, *Education, the Practice of Freedom* (Writers and Readers 1976; first published in Brazil 1967)

Freire, Paulo, *Pedagogy of the Oppressed* (Penguin 1972; first published in USA 1970)

Freire, Paulo, *Pedagogy in Progress* (Writers and Readers 1978)

Fromm, Erich, *Fear of Freedom*

Gaine, C., *No Problem Here* (Hutchinson 1987)

Gardener, D.E.M., *Experiment and Tradition in Primary Schools* (Methuen 1966)

Gardener, D.E.M., *Susan Isaacs* (1969)

Gardener, Phil, *The Lost Elementary Schools of Victorian England* (Croom Helm 1984)

Gilchrist, Linda see Chanan, Gabriel

Gibson, Tony, *Youth for Freedom* (Freedom Press 1951)

Gill, D and Levidow, L (eds), *Anti-Racist Science Teaching* (Free Association Books 1987)

Gilroy, P., *There Ain't No Black in the Union Jack* (Hutchinson 1988)

Gintis, Herbert, see Bowles, Samuel

Giroud, Gabriel, *Cempius: Education Integrale* (Paris: Schleicher 1900)

Giroud, Gabriel, *Paul Robin: Sa Vie, Ses Idees, Son Action* (Paris: G. Migrolet et Starz 1937)

Godwin, William, *Enquiry Concerning Political Justice* (1946)

Godwin, William, *The Enquirer: Reflections on Education, Manners and Literature* [1797] (facsimile edition: New York: Augustus M.Kelley 1964)

Godwin, William, *Fleetwood: or, The New Man of Feeling* (London 1805)

Godwin, William, *An Account of the Seminary* [1783] (reprinted in Four Early Pamphlets 1783-4, ed. Pollin, B.R., Gainesville 1966)

Goldman, Emma, *Red Emma Speaks: Selected Writings and Speeches By Emma Goldman* (compiled and editted by Alix Kates Schuman) (Wildwood House 1979)

Goldman, Emma, *Anarchism and Other Essays* (New York: Mother Earth Publishing, 1911)

Goodman, Paul, *Compulsory Miseducation* (Penguin 1971; first published in USA 1962)

Goodman, Paul, *Growing Up Absurd* (Gollancz 1961; first published in USA 1960)

Gordon, Tuula, *Democracy in One School* (Brighton: Falmer Press 1986)

Graubard, Allen, *Free the Children* (New York: Vintage Books 1974)

Greenslade, R., *Goodbye to the Working Class*

Gribble, David, *Considering Children* (Dorling Kindersley 1985)

Gribble, David, *That's All Folks* (Newton Abbot: Town and Country Books)

Gross, Ronald and Gross, Beatrice, *Radical School Reform* (Gollancz 1971; first published in USA 1969)

Grosskurth, P., *Havelock Ellis* (Allen Lane, The Penguin Press 1980)

Grunsell, Rob, *Absent From School* (Writers and Readers)

Hall, John R., *The Ways Out: Utopian Communal Groups in an Age of Babylon* (RKP 1978)

Hansen, Saxaren and Jensen, Jasper, *The Little Red Schoolbook* (Stage1, 1971)

Harber, Clive, Meighan, Roland and Roberts, Brian (eds), *Alternative Educational Futures* (Holt, Rinehart and Winston 1984)

Harber, Clive, and Meighan, Roland (eds), *The Democratic School* (Education Now 1988)

Hardy, Denis, *Alternative Communities in 19th Century England* (Longman 1979)

Head, David (ed), *Free Way to Learning* (Penguin 1974)

Hemmings, Ray, *Fifty Years of Freedom* (George Allen and Unwin 1972)

Hemmings, Ray and others, *The Only Interruption in My Education Was When I Went to School* (A.S.Neill Trust 1978)

Henry, Jules, *Culture Against Man* (Penguin 1972; first published in USA 1963)

Henry, Jules, *Essays on Education* (Penguin 1971)

Herndon, James, *The Way It Spozed to Be* (Pitman 1970)

Hoggart, Richard, *The Uses of Literacy* (Chatto and Windus 1957)

Holly, Douglas, *Beyond Curriculum* (Hart-Davis MacGibbon 1973)

Holly, Douglas (ed), *Education or Domination* (Arrow Books 1974)

Holly, Douglas, *Society, Schools and Humanity* (MacGibbon and Kee 1971)

Holmes, Edmond, *Give Me the Young* (Constable 1921)

Holmes, Edmond, *In Defence of What Might Be* (Constable 1914)

Holmes, Edmond, *The Tragedy of Education* (Constable 1913)

Holmes, Edmond, *What Is and What Might Be* (Constable 1911)

Holmes, Gerard, *The Idiot Teacher* (Faber 1952)

Holt, John, *Escape from Childhood* (Penguin 1975)

Holt, John, *Freedom and Beyond* (Penguin 1973; first published in USA 1972)

Holt, John, *How Children Fail* (Pitman 1965; first published in USA 1964)

Holt, John, *How Children Learn* (Penguin 1970; first published in USA 1967)

Holt, John, *Instead of Education* (Penguin 1977)

Holt, John, *The Underachieving School* (Penguin 1971; first published in USA 1970)

Holt, John, *What Do I Do Monday?* (Pitman 1971; first published in USA 1970)

Holton, Bob, *British Syndicalism 1900-14* (1977)

Hornsey College of Art, Staff and Students of, *The Hornsey Affair* (Penguin 1969)

Hoyles, Martin (ed), *Changing Childhood* (Writers and Readers1979)

Hoyles, Martin, *The Politics of Childhood* (Journeyman 1988)

Hoyles, Martin (ed), *The Politics of Literacy* (Writers and Readers 1977)

Hudson, Liam, *Contrary Imaginations* (Methuen 1966)

Humphrey, S., *Hooligans and Rebels* (1979)

Illich, Ivan, *The Alternative to Schooling* (Student Christian Movement undated)

Illich, Ivan, *After Deschooling, What?* (Writers and Readers 1974)

Illich, Ivan, *Deschooling Society* (Calder and Boyars 1971)

Illich, Ivan, *Disabling Professions* (Marion Boyars 1977)

Illich, Ivan and Verne, Etienne, *Imprisoned in the Global Classroom* (Writers and Readers 1976)

Isaacs, Susan, *Intellectual Growth in Young Children* (Routledge 1930)

Isaacs, Susan, *Social Development in Young Children* (Routledge 1933)

Isaacs, Susan, *The Children We Teach* (University of London Press 1932)

Isaacs, Susan, *The Nursery Years* (Routledge 1929)

Jackson, Brian and Marsden, Dennis, *Education and the Working Class* [1962] (Penguin 1966)

Jensen, Jasper see Hansen, Saxaren

Joll, J., *The Anarchists* (Eyre and Spottiswood 1964)

Jones, Ken, *Beyond Progressive Education* (Macmillan 1983)

Jones, Ken, *Right Turn* (Hutchinson 1989)

Jones, Richard M., *Fantasy and Feeling in Education* (Penguin1972)

Kamin, Leon, *The Science and Politics of IQ* (Penguin 1977)

Keddie, Nell (ed), *Tinker,Tailor... The Myth of Cultural Deprivation* (Penguin 1973)

Kohl, Herbert, *36 Children* (Gollancz 1968; first published in USA 1967)

Kohl, Herbert, *The Open Classroom* (Methuen 1970; first published in USA 1969)

Kohl, Herbert, *Reading: How To* (Penguin)

Kozol, Jonathan, *Death at an Early Age* (Penguin 1968; first published in USA 1967)

Kozol, Jonathan, *Free Schools* (Boston: Houghton Miflin 1972)

Kropotkin, Peter, *Kropotkin's Revolutionary Pamphlets* (New York: Dover Publications 1970)

Lambert, Jack and Pearson, Jenny, *Adventure Playgrounds* (Penguin 1974)

Lane, Homer, *Talks to Parents and Teachers* (Allen and Unwin 1928)

Le Guin, Ursula, *The Dispossessed* (Grafton 1986)

Leberstein, Stephen, *Revolutionary Education: French Libertarian Theory and Experiments 1895-1915* (University of Wisconsin PhD Dissertation 1972)

Lee-Wright, Peter, *Child Slaves* (Earthscan 1990)

Leicester, M., *Multicultural Education* (NFER-Nelson 1989)

Lipansky, Edmond-Marc, *La Pedagogie Libertaire* (Paris: Zero de Conduite 1986)

Lister, Ian, (ed) *Deschooling* (Cambridge University Press 1974)

McCallister, W.J., *The Growth of Freedom in Education* (1931)

Mackenzie, R.F., *Escape from the Classroom* (Collins 1965)

Mackenzie, R.F., *A Question of Living* (Collins 1963)

Mackenzie, R.F., *The Sins of the Children* (Collins 1967)

Mackenzie, R.F., *State School* (Penguin 1970)

Mackenzie, R.F., *The Unbowed Head* (Edinburgh University Student Publications Board 1977)

McMillan, Margaret, *The Child and the State* (National LabourPress 1911)

McMillan, Margaret, *Early Childhood* (1900)

McMillan, Margaret, *Education Through the Imagination* (1904)

McMillan, Margaret, *Labour and Childhood* (1907)

MacMunn, Norman, *The Child's Path to Freedom* (Bell 1914)

MacMunn, Norman, *A Path to Freedom in the School* (Bell 1921)

Makarenko, Anton, *The Road to Life* (Stanley Nott 1936)

Mannin, Ethel, *Commonsense and the Child* (Jarrolds 1930)

Mannin, Ethel, *Commonsense and the Adolescent* (Jarrolds 1938)

Marshall, P. (ed), *The Anarchist Writings of William Godwin* (Freedom Press 1986)

Marson, Dave, *Children's Strikes in 1911* (History Workshop 1973)

Meighan, Roland, *Flexi-Schooling* (Education Now 1989)

Members of the Internationale Situationniste and Students of Strasbourg, *On the Poverty of Student Life* (Dark Star/Rebel Press 1985)

Mildiner, Leslie and House, Bill, *The Gates* (Centerprise 1975)

Miles, R., *Racism* (Routledge 1989)

Montessori, Maria, *A Montessori Handbook* (ed R.C. Orem: NewYork: Capricorn Books 1966)

Montessori, Maria, *The Discovery of the Child* (1948)

Montessori, Maria, *The Secret of Childhood* (Bombay: Orient Longmans 1936)

Moon, Bob (ed), *Comprehensive Schools: Challenge and Change* (NFER Nelson 1983)

National Council for Civil Liberties, *Rights of Children* (NCCL 1972)

Nearing, Scott, *Education in Soviet Russia* (Plebs League 1926)

Muncie, J., *The Trouble With Kids Today* (Hutchinson 1984)

Neill, A.S., *A Dominie's Log* (Herbert Jenkins 1915)

Neill, A.S., *A Dominie Dismissed* (Herbert Jenkins 1916)

Neill, A.S., *The Booming of Bunkie* (Herbert Jenkins 1919)

Neill, A.S., *A Dominie in Doubt* (Herbert Jenkins 1921)

Neill, A.S., *Carroty Broon* (Herbert Jenkins 1921)

Neill, A.S., *A Dominie Abroad* (Herbert Jenkins 1923)

Neill, A.S., *A Dominie's Five* (Herbert Jenkins 1924)

Neill, A.S., *The Problem Child* (Herbert Jenkins 1926)

Neill, A.S., *The Problem Parent* (Herbert Jenkins 1932)

Neill, A.S., *Is Scotland Educated?* (Routledge 1936)
Neill, A.S., *That Dreadful School* (Herbert Jenkins 1937)
Neill, A.S., *The Last Man Alive...* (Herbert Jenkins 1938)
Neill, A.S., *The Problem Teacher* (Herbert Jenkins 1939)
Neill, A.S., *Hearts Not Heads in the School* (Herbert Jenkins 1945)
Neill, A.S., *The Problem Family* (Herbert Jenkins 1949)
Neill, A.S., *The Free Child* (Herbert Jenkins 1953)
Neill, A.S., *Freedom Not License!* (New York: Hart 1966)
Neill, A.S., *Summerhill* (Penguin 1968)
Neill, A.S., *Summerhill: A Radical Approach to Education* (Gollancz 1962)
Neill, A.S., *Talking of Summerhill* (Gollancz 1967)
Neill, A.S., *Neill! Neill! Orange Peel!: A Personal View of Ninety Years* (Wiedenfeld and Nicholson 1973)
Neill, A.S. and Ritter, P., *Wilhelm Reich* (Ritter Press 1958)
Otty, Nicholas, *Learner Teacher* (Penguin 1972)
Park, J., *Bertrand Russell on Education* (Allen and Unwin 1964)
Parkhurst, H., *Education on the Dalton Plan* (1923)
Paton, Keith, *The Great Brain Robbery* (Keith Paton 1971)
Paul, Leslie, *The Republic of Children* (Allen and Unwin 1938)
Pearse, Innes and Crocker, Lucy H., *The Peckham Experiment* (Allen and Unwin 1943)
Pekin, L.B., *Progressive Schools* (Hogarth Press 1934)
Perry, Leslie (ed), *Four Progressive Educators* (Collier-MacMillan 1967)
Pestalozzi, J.H., *How Gertrude Teaches Her Children* [1801]
Pestalozzi, J.H., *Leonard and Gertrude* [1787] (Boston: D.C.Heath and Co. 1898)
Popenue, Joseph, *Inside Summerhill* (New York: Hart 1969)
Postman, Neil and Weingartner, Charles, *Teaching as a Subversive Activity* (Penguin 1971; first published in USA 1969)
Progressive Labor Party, *Racism, IQ and the Class Society* (American Progressive Labor Party; reprinted by Campaign on Racism, IQ and the Class Society and Humpty Dumpty 1972)
Punch, Maurice, *Progressive Retreat* (Cambridge University Press 1977)
Quick, R.H., *Essays on Educational Reformers* (Longman 1910)
Rank and File, *Democracy in Schools* (Rank and File 1971)
Rawson, W., *The Freedom We Seek* (New Education Foundation 1937)
Raynaud, J.M. and Ambauves, Guy, *L'Education Libertaire* (Paris: Spartacus 1978)
Read, Herbert, *Education Through Art* (Faber 1961)
Reich, Wilhelm, *The Mass Psychology of Fascism* (Penguin 1970)
Reich, Wilhelm, *Sex-Pol: Essays 1929-1934* (edited by Lee Baxandall) (New York: Random House 1972)
Reimer, Everett, *School Is Dead* (Penguin 1971)
Revell, Dorothy, *Cheiron's Cave*
Ritter, P. and Ritter, J., *Free Family and Feedback* (Gollancz 1959)
Rocker, Rudolf, *The London Years* (Robert Anscombe 1956)
Rogers, Carl, *Freedom to Learn* (Columbus, Ohio: Merrill 1969)
Rogers, Carl, *On Becoming A Person* (Constable 1961)
Rosen, Harold, *Language and Class* (Falling Wall Press 1972)
Rousseau, Jean-Jacques, *Emile* [1762] (J.M.Dent 1911)
Rowland, Stephen, *The Enquiring Classroom* (Brighton: Falmer Press 1984)
Rubinstein, David and Stoneman, Colin (eds), *Education for Democracy* (first edition: Penguin 1970; second edition: Penguin 1972)
Rubinstein, David (ed), *Education and Equality* (Penguin 1979)
Rugg, H. and Shumaker, Ann, *The Child-Centred School* (Yonkers: World Book Co 1928)
Russell, Bertrand, *Autobiography Volume II* (Allen and Unwin 1968)

Russell, Bertrand, *Education and the Social Order* (Allen and Unwin 1968)

Russell, Bertrand, *On Education* (Allen and Unwin 1926)

Russell, Bertrand, *Principles of Social Reconstruction* (Allen and Unwin 1916)

Russell, Bertrand, *Unpopular Essays* (Unwin 1976)

Russell, Dora, *The Tamarisk Tree* (Elek Penlenton 1975)

Russell, Dora, *The Tamarisk Tree 2: My School and the Years of War* (Virago 1980)

Rust, Val D., *Alternatives in Education* (Sage 1977)

Schonhaus, W., *The Dark Places of Education* (Allen and Unwin 1932)

Schools Without Walls, *Lunatic Ideas* (Schools Without Walls/CornerHouse Bookshop 1978)

Schwartz, B.N. (ed), *Affirmative Education* (New Jersey: Prentice- Hall 1972)

Scott-Samuel, Alex (ed), *Total Participation, Total Health, Reinventing the Peckham Health Centre for the 1990s* (Scottish Academy Press 1990)

Searle, Chris (compiler), *Classrooms of Resistance* (Writers and Readers 1975)

Searle, Chris (compiler), *The World in a Classroom* (Writers and Readers 1977)

Searle, Chris, *This New Season* (Calder and Boyars 1973)

Segefjord, Bjarne, *Summerhill Diary* (Gollancz 1971)

Selleck, R.J.W., *English Primary Education and the Progressives 1914-1939* (RKP 1972)

Selleck, R.J.W., *The New Education 1870-1914* (Pitman 1968)

Shaw, B., *Misalliance with a Treatise on Parents and Children* (Constable 1919)

Shaw, Nellie, *Whiteway: A Colony on the Cotswolds* (C.W.Daniel 1935)

Shaw, Otto, *Maladjusted Boys* (Allen and Unwin 1965)

Silberman, Charles, *Crisis in the Classroom* (New York: Vintage Books 1971)

Silver, Harold, *English Education and the Radicals 1780-1850* (RKP 1975)

Simon, Brian, *Bending the Rules* (Lawrence and Wishart 1988)

Simon, Brian, *Education and the Labour Movement 1870-1920* (Lawrence and Wishart 1965)

Simon, Brian (ed), *The Radical Tradition in Education in Britain* (Lawrence and Wishart 1972)

Simon, Brian, *Intelligence Testing and the Comprehensive School* (Lawrence and Wishart 1953)

Simpson, J.H., *Sane Schools*

Skidelsky, R., *English Progressive Schools* (Penguin 1969)

Smith, Michael P., *The Libertarians and Education* (Allen and Unwin 1983)

Smith, Michael, *The Underground and Education* (Methuen 1977)

Snell, Reginald, *St. Christopher's School 1915-75* (Aldine Press 1975)

Snitzer, Herb, *Summerhill: A Loving World* (Macmillan 1964)

Spock, Benjamin, *The Common Sense Book of Baby and Child Care* [1946] (J. Lane 1955)

Spring, Joel, *A Primer of Libertarian Education* (New York: FreeLife Editions 1975)

Stallibrass, Alison, *Being Me and Also Us - Lessons from the Peckham Experiment* (Scottish Academy Press 1989)

Stallibrass, Alison, *The Self-Respecting Child* [1974] (Addison-Wesley 1989)

Standing, E.M., *Maria Montessori: Her Life and Work* (New York: New American Library 1962)

Steiner, Rudolf, *Education and Modern Spiritual Life* (Anthroposophical Publishing Centre)

Stewart, W.A.C., *Progressives and Radicals in English Education 1750-1970* (Macmillan 1972)

Stewart, W.A.C., *The Educational Innovators, Volume 2: Progressive Schools 1881-1967* (Macmillan 1968)

Stewart, W.A.C. and McCann, W.P., *The Educational Innovators 1750-1880* (Macmillan 1967)

Stirner, Max, *The False Principles of Our Education* (Colorado Springs: Ralph Myles 1967)

Stoneman, Colin, see Rubinstein, David

Students and Staff, *The Hornsey Affair* (Penguin 1969)

Tawney, R.H., *Equality* (Allen and Unwin 1931)

Tawney, R.H., *Secondary Education for All* (Allen and Unwin 1922)

Thomas, Edith, *Louise Michel* (Montreal: Black Rose Books 1981)

Thompson, E.P., *Warwick University Ltd.* (Penguin 1970)

Tolstoy, Leo, *Tolstoy on Education* (Chicago: University of Chicago Press 1967)

Toogood, Philip, *The Head's Tale* (Dialogue 1984)

Troyat, H., *Tolstoy* (Penguin 1970)

Van der Eyken, William and Turner, Barry, *Adventures in Education* (Penguin 1975)

Verne, Etienne, see Illich, Ivan

Waller, Willard, *The Sociology of Teaching* [1933] (New York: John Wiley 1965)

Walmsley, John and Berg, Leila, *Neill and Summerhill: A Man and His Work* (Penguin 1969)

Walvin, James, *A Child's World* (Penguin 1982)

Ward, Colin, *Anarchy in Action* (Freedom Press 1982)

Ward, Colin, *The Child in the City* (The Architectural Press 1978)

Ward, Colin and Fyson, Anthony, *Streetwork: The Exploding School* (RKP 1973)

Washburn, Carleton, *Schools Aren't What They Were* (Heinemann 1953)

Watts, John (ed), *The Countesthorpe Experience* (Allen and Unwin 1977)

Weeks, A., *Comprehensive Schools: Past, Present and Future* (Methuen 1986)

White Lion Street Free School, *Bulletins 2 to 5* (WLSFS 1972-1980)

White Lion Street Free School, *How To Set Up A Free School* (WLSFS 1973)

Whitty, Geoff and Young. Michael (eds) *Explorations in the Politics of School Knowledge* (Nafferton Books 1976)

Whyld, Janie, Pickersgill, Dave and Jackson, David (eds) *Update on Anti-Sexist Work with Boys and Young Men* (Whyld Publishing Coop, 1990)

Williams, Raymond, *The Long Revolution* (Chatto and Windus 1961)

Wills, W. David, *The Barns Experiment* (Allen and Unwin 1945)

Wills, W. David, *The Hawkspur Experiment* (Allen and Unwin 1967)

Wills, W. David, *Homer Lane: A Biography* (Allen and Unwin 1964)

Wills, W. David, *Throw Away The Rod* (Gollancz 1960)

Woods, Alice, *Educational Experiments in England* (Methuen 1920)

Wollstonecraft, Mary, *Vindication of the Rights of Women* [1792] (Penguin 1975)

Wright, Nigel, *Assessing Radical Education* (Open University Press 1989)

Wright, Nigel, *Free School: The White Lion Experiment* (Libertarian Education 1989)

Wright, Nigel, *Progress in Education* (Croom Helm 1977)

Young, Michael, *The Elmhirsts of Dartington: The Creation of a Utopian Community* (RKP 1982)

Zeldin, D., *The Educational Ideas of Charles Fourier* (1772-1837) (Frank Cass 1969)

We are very grateful to Nigel Wright for compiling this bibliography. For a fairly comprehensive list of radical pamphlets and periodicals, see the bibliography in his book, *Assessing Radical Education*.

Lib ED Subject Index

Lib ED magazine has run to almost 50 issues so far. Some of the back issues are still in print, and photocopies are available of those that have sold out.

Titles are indexed by Volume (I,II), Issue Number (1-30) and Page.

PLAY AND LEISURE

PRE-SCHOOL

PSYCHOLOGY

RACISM

RESOURCES

SCHOOLS

SCIENCE, MATHS AND TECHNOLOGY

SELECTION

SEX AND SEXUALITY

SEXISM

SEXUAL ABUSE

SPECIAL NEEDS

STATE REFORMS

TRUANCY

UNIONS AND ACTION

VICTIMISATION

Directory

A directory of groups and organisations...

A Distribution,
84b Whitechapel High Street,
London E1 7QX,
081-558-7732.
(Distributor of Anarchist books and
magazines)

Advisory Centre for Education,
18 Victoria Park Square,
London E2,
081-980-4596.

Advisory Service for Squatters,
2 St. Paul's Road,
London N1.

Afro-Caribbean Education Resource
Project,
Wyvil Road School,
Wyvil Road,
London SW8
071-627-2662.

AIMER,
Faculty of Education and Community
Studies,
The University of Reading,
Bulmershe Court,
Earley,
Reading RG6 1HY.
(a database of resources on a full range
of curriculum areas and topics)

AK Distribution,
3 Balmoral Place,
Stirling,
Scotland FK8 2RD.
(Mail order for libertarian/anarchist
books and publications, write for a
catalogue)

All London Teachers Against Racism and
Fascism,
Panther House,
Room 216,
38 Mount Pleasant
London WC1.

Animal Aid,
7 Castle Street,
Tonbridge,
Kent TN9 1BH.

Animal Liberation Front Supporters
Group,
BCM 1160,
London WC1N 3XX.
(for those not directly involved but who
want to support the work of the ALF)

Anti-Apartheid Movement,
13 Mandela Street,
London NW1 0DW.
071-387-7966.

Anti-Fascist Action,
PO Box 273,
Forest Gate, London E7.
071-387-2531.

Association of Teachers of Mathematics
(ATM),
Kings Chambers,
Queen Street,
Derby DE1 3DA.

Black and in Care,
20 Compton Terrace,
London N1 2UN.
(for black young people in care)

Black Flag/Anarchist Black Cross,
BM Hurricane,
London WC1N 3XX.
(anarchist monthly and prisoners
support organisation)

Bread'n'Roses/Tenants' Corner
46a Oval Mansions
Vauxhall Street,
London SE11.
01-582-7286.
(housing and education resource centre
run by tenants)

British Union for the Abolition of
Vivisection,
162 Crane Grove,
London N7 8LB.
(publishes *Liberator* and have many
resource packs)

Buktu African/Caribbean Education and
Training Resource Centre,
138 Grosvenor Road,
Bristol BS2 8YA.
(includes a supplementary school for
black students)

Campaign Against Military Research on
Campus (CAMROC),
190 Burdett Road,
London E3 4AA.
081-980-2455.

Centre for Alternative Technology,
Machynlleth,
Powys,
Wales.

Children's Home-Based Education
Association,
14 Basil Avenue,
Amthorpe,
Doncaster DN3 2AT.
0302-833596.
(support organisation for children out of
school and their families)

Children's Legal Centre,
20 Compton Terrrace,
London N1 2UN.
071-359-6251.

Commonweal Collection,
c/o JB Priestley Library,
University of Bradford,
Bradford BD7 1DP.
(a small library for anybody interested in
libertarian, anarchist or pacifist ideas)

Co-ordinating Animal Welfare,
PO Box 589,
Bristol BS99 1RW.
(publishes *CAW Bulletin*, have a free
video lending library and lots of info on
all aspects of animal abuse)

Daycare Trust,
Wesley House,
4 Wild Court,
London WC2B 5AU.

Education Otherwise,
25 Common Lane,
Hemmingford Abbots,
Cambridgeshire.
(for everybody who practices or supports
the right of children to learn without
schooling)

EPOCH - End Physical Punishment of
Children,
PO Box 962,
London N22 4UX.
(campaigning for the end of physical
punishment of children by parents and
other carers)

Feminist Library,
5/50 Westminster Bridge Road,
London SE1.
071-928-7789.

Forest School Camps,
Lorna English (secretary)
110 Burbage Road,
London SE24 9HD.
(an organisation that organises camps
for children)

Freedom,
Angel Alley,
84b. Whitechapel High Street,
London E1 7QX.
01-247-9249.
(anarchist fortnightly, book publisher
and bookshop)

Gay Youth Help Service,
37 Rosenthal House,
45 Rushey Green,
London SE6 4AR.
081-698-2857.

Global Futures Project,
Institute of Education,
University of London,
10 Woburn Square,
London WC1H 0NS.

Green College,
c/o Peter de la Cour,
17 Western Road,
Oxford OX1 4LF.
0865-249020.
(independent international college which
promotes eco-centrist values)

Human Scale Education Movement,
96 Carlingcott,
Bath BA2 8AW.
0761-33733

Hummingbird Multicultural Resources,
24 Ashley Hill,
Montpelier,
Bristol BS6 5JG.
0272-541946.
(publish a mail order catalogue of books
and other resources)

In From The Cold,
c/o 49 Cabrera Avenue,
Virginia Water,
Surrey GU25 4HA.

Intermediate Technology Developmnent
Group,
Myson House,
Railway Terrace,
Rugby CV21 3HT.

International Association for the Child's
Right to Play,
Paul Soames, UK Branch Secretary,
Contact-a-Family,
15 Strutton Ground,
London SW1 P2HP.

Kidscape,
82 Brooke Road,,
London W1Y 1WG.
('Good sense defence' against sexual
abuse for the young. Materials and
courses for schools, adults and children)

Leaveners Experimental Arts Project,
Legard Works,
Legard Road,
Highbury,
London N5 1DE.
071-226-8025.
(theatre for teenagers)

Lesbian and Gay Workers in Education,
BM Gay Teacher,
London WC1N 3XX.
071-837-7234.

Lesbian and Gay Youth Movement,
BM G.Y.M.,
London WC1N 3XX.
081-317-9690.

Letterbox Library,
8 Bradbury Street,
London N16 8JN.
071-254-1640.
(non-sexist and multi-cultural book club
for children, write or phone for their free
catalogue)

Libertarian Network of People with
Disabilities,
c/o Townsend House,
Green Lanes,
Marshfield,
Chippenham,
Wiltshire.

Minority Rights Group,
29 Craven Street,
London WC2N 5NG.
071-930-6659.

National Anti-Vivisection Society,
51 Hawley Street,
London W1N 1DD.
(publishes *The Campaigner*, and some
excellent stuff for kids)

National Council for Civil Liberties,
21 Tabbard Street,
London SE1 4LA.
(many resource packs and reading lists)

National Secular Society,
702 Holloway Road,
London N19.
071-272-1266.

National Youth Bureau,
17-23 Albion Street,
Leicester LE1 6GD.
0533-471200.

New Education Directory,
15 Belle Vue,
Clifton,
Bristol BS8 1DB.
0272-735091.

New Games UK,
PO Box 542,
London NW2 3PQ.

New Grapevine,
416 St. John's Street,
London EC1.
071-278-9147.

Off Centre Gallery,
13 Cotswold Road,
Bristol BS3 4NX.
(independent and innovative art gallery)

Outsiders Club,
Box 4ZB,
London W1A 4ZB.
071-499-0900
(a self-help group which encourages the
exploration of sexuality and relationship
problems)

Peace Education Project,
Peace Pledge Union,
6 Endsleigh Street,
London WC1.
071-387-5501.

Play For Life,
31b. Ipswich Road,
Norwich,
NR2 2LN.
(life affirming toys for children)

Post-Adoption Centre
Gregory House,
48 Mecklenburgh Square,
London WC1.

Pre-School Playgroups Association,
61-63 Kings Cross Road,
London WC1X.
071-833-0991.

Radical Alternatives to Prison,
BCM Box 4842,
London WC1N 3XX.
(publish *The Abolitionist*, school
discussion packs and will do talks)

Radical Routes Network,
c/o 24 South Road,
Hockley,
Birmingham
(network of alternative communities)

Release,
071-377-5905.
(legal help with drug problems)

The Science Exploratory,
The Old Station,
Temple Meads,
Bristol BS1 6QU.
0272-252008.
(hands-on science exhibition)

Scottish Civil Liberty Trust,
146 Holland Street,
Glasgow G2 4NG.
(provides legal information and has
published a series of leaflets for young
people in Scotland)

Shocking Pink,
Young Women's Magazine Collective,
23 Tunstall Road,
Brixton,
London SW9 8BZ.

Skool Bus Project,
24 Clive Street,
Hereford HR1 2SB.
(education for children of travellers)

Society of Teachers Opposed to Physical Punishment.
18 Victoria Park Square,
London E2.
081-980-8523.

Steiner Schools Fellowship,
Orlingbury House,
Lewes Road,
Forest Row,
Sussex RH18 5AA.
0342-822115.

Surrey Library of Teaching Resources for International Understanding, Justice and Peace,
6 Phoenix Cottages,
Dorking Road,
Bookham,
Surrey KT23 4QG.
0372-56421
(mail order service with massive catalogue)

Taboo Support Groups for Incest Survivors,
PO Box 38,
Manchester M60 1HG.

Teachers For Animal Rights,
c/o Wanda Dejlidko,
29 Lynwood Road,
London SW17.

Terrence Higgins Trust,
071-242-1010 (daily helpline)
071-831-0330 (mon-Fri 10-6).
(for those worried about HIV/AIDS)

University of the Third Age,
Wren Street,
London WC1.
071-833-4747.
(educational groups for older learners)

Woodcraft Folk,
13 Ritherton Road,
London SW17.
081-672-6031.
(a kind of non-sexist, non-militarist scouts and brownies)

World Action for Recyling Materials and Energy from Rubbish (WARMER campaign),
83 Mt Ephraim,
Tunbridge Wells,
Kent TN4 8BS.
0892-24626
(independent world-wide service to encourage the recycling of materials and energy from consumer waste)

World Studies Journal,
World Studies Teacher Training Centre,
University of York,
Heslington,
York YO1 5DD.

World University Service,
20 Compton Terrace,
London N1 2UN.
(promotes education for international development)

World Wildlife Fund UK Education Department,
Panda House,
Weyside Park,
Goldalming,
Surrey GU7 1XR.
0483-426444.

Workers Educational Association,
9 Upper Berkeley Street,
London W1H.
071-402-5608.

Youth For Animal Rights,
112-126 Camden High Street,
London NW1 0LU.
071-485-5857.

Z to A Project,
24 South Road,
Hockley,
Birmingham B18.
021-551-1679.
(formerly New University - an alternative learning project)

Zoo Check,
Cherry Tree Cottage,
Coldharbour,
Surrey RH5 6HA.

SCHOOLS OF INTEREST

Britain

Bath Place School,
Bath Place Community Venture,
Bath Place,
Leamington.
(education for 16-year-olds who have
removed themselves from school)

Blackcurrent Otherwise Project,
132 St. James Park Road,
Northampton NN5 5EL.
(a living/learning project)

Countesthorpe College,
Winchester Road,
Coutesthorpe,
Leicestershire.
(state community college, for 14-18 yr
olds)

Kilquhanity House School,
Castle Douglas,
Kircudbrightshire,
Scotland.
(free school for childen 4-18 yrs old, day
or residential)

Kirkdale Free School Project,
c/o 11 Veronica Road,
Upper Tooting,
London SW17 8QL.
(in hibernation at the moment, but
raring to get out)

Rowen House School,
Holbrook Road,
Belper,
Derbyshire DE5 1PB.
(for girls under stress)

Sands School,
48 East Street,
Ashburton,
Devon.
(for children 11-16)

Skool Bus Project,
24 Clive Street,
Hereford HR1 2SB.
(a travelling bus for travellers' children)

Summerhill School,
Leiston,
Suffolk.
(probably the world's most famous free
school, founded by A. S. Neill)

Dame Catherines School,
Ticknall,
Derbyshire.

The Small School,
Hartland,
Devon.
(two independent non fee-paying schools
associated with the Human Scale
Education Movement)

The Sutton Centre,
Sutton-in-Ashfield,
Nottinghamshire.
(state school for 11-18 year olds,
combined with a leisure and amenity
centre)

International Directory

Argentina

Grupo Impulso Libertario,
CC984,
200 Rosario,
Republic of Argentina.

Australia

Connect,
12, Brooke Street,
Northcote 3070,
Victoria,
Australia.

Austria

Free Schools in Vienna,
c/o Davidgasse 6/15,
1100 Wien,
Austria.

Botswana

Foundation of Education with
Production,
PO Box 20906,
Gaborone,
Botswana.
(education for social change)

Canada

Syndicat des Eleves,
2035 Boulevard St-Laurent,
Montreal,
Quebec,
Canada.

Denmark

Dansk Friskoleforening,
Prices Havevej 11,
DK-5600 Faaborg.
010-45-62-613013
(association which represents 183 free
schools with 17,000 students)

Hojskolens Sekretariat,
Farvergade 27G,
DK-1463 Kobenhavn K.
(Folk High School secretariat)

Lilleskolernes Sammenslutning,
Skjoerringvej 25,
DK-8464 Galten.
010-45-86-944281
(association which represents 41 schools,
most of which have a critical, left-wing,
attitude to the established society)

France

Apprendre Autrement,
Marcel Malk,
31 Route de Toulouse,
L'isle de Dodon,
France.

Association Nationale pour l'Education
Nouvelle,
1 Rue des Nefliers,
31400 Toulouse,
France.

Le CERISE,
77 Rue des Haies,
75020 Paris,
France.

Circule-Air,
Agence Informations Enfance,
29 Rue Davy,
75017 Paris,
France.

Les Enfants D'abord,
Mas de Grands Pan,
Gimeaux,
13200 Arles,
France.

Germany

Padagogik-Kooperative e.V.
Goebenstrasse 8
2800 Bremen
tel: 0421 3449 29
(organisation of Freinet educationalists)

India

ANKUR,
J-21, Hauz Khas Enclave,
New Dehli 110016,
India.
tel: 661473.
(society for alternatives in education)

Italy

Centro Studi Libertari,
Via Rovetta 27,
20127 Milano,
Italy.

Edizioni Anarchismo,
Casello Postale 61,
95100 Catania,
Italy.

Spain

Asamblea Libertaria de Ensenanza,
Apdo 14218,
08080 Barcelona,
Spain.

Asociacion Pedagogica Paideia,
Alvaro 21,
06800 Merida,
Spain.

CNT-AIT Ensenyament,
Calle Unio 16,
1-1 Barcelona 08001,
Spain.
tel: 301-06-12.

CNT-Federacio d'Ensenyament de
Catalunya,
c/o Roger de Lluria,
123 Pral,
08037 Barcelona
tel: 215-13-64 or 215-19-83.

Estudiantes Anarquistas,
Apdo 385,
10080 Caceres,
Spain.

Sweden

KAP (Kooperativet Arbetets Pedagogik),
Slupskjulsvagen B 103,
S 111 49 Stockholm
Sweden.
tel: 08/21-30-67.

KRUT (Kritisk Utbildnings Tidskrift),
Torpedverkstaden,
Skeppsholmen,
S 111 49 Stockholm,
Sweden.
tel: 08/21-70-10
(critical journal of education)

SAC (Syndikalisterna),
Sveavagen 98,
S 113 50 Stockholm,
Sweden.
tel: 08/34-35-59.

Switzerland

Centre International de Recherches sur
l'Anarchisme (CIRA),
Avenue de Beaumont 24,
CH-1012 Lausanne,
Switzerland.
tel: 021-32 48 19 or 021-32 35 43.
(The library is open every weekday from
4 to 7 pm (or by appointment). Loans,
bibliographies, information and other
services are available for readers who
have paid the annual subscription (at
present SF40, US$25, £15)

U.S.A.

Aero-gramme,
417 Roslyn Road,
Roslyn Heights,
NY 11577,
USA.
tel: 516 621-2195.
(an alternative education resource
organisation newsletter)

Growing Without Schooling,
2269 Massachusetts Avenue,
Cambridge,
MA 02140,
U.S.A.
(US equivalent of Education Otherwise)

National Coalition of Alternative
Community Schools,
58 Schoolhouse Road,
Summertown,
TN 38483
U.S.A.
tel: 615-964 3670.

Rethinking Schools,
1001 East Keefe Avenue,
Milwauwee,
Wisconsin 53212
U.S.A.
(magazine which re-thinks schools)

INTERNATIONAL SCHOOLS OF INTEREST

Australia

Acrobatic Arts Community School,
PO Box 1101,
Wodonga 3690,
Australia.

Kensington Community High School
393 Macauley road,
Kensington 3031,
Australia

Marbury School,
160 Mt Barker Road,
Aldgate
SA 5154,
Australia.
(postal address:
Box 396,
Stirling,
SA 5152,
Australia.)

Austria

Schulerschule,
WUK,
Wahringerstrasse 59,
1090 Wien,
Austria.
(a co-educational, non-sectarian,
independent, non-competitive,
non-authoritarian boarding school)

Belgium

De Weide Free School,
Sevekootstraat 67,
Erpe-mere,
Nr. Aalst,
Belgium.

Denmark

Brenderup Folkehosjkole,
Nordisk Fredhojskole,
Stationsvej 54,
DK-5464 Brenderup,
Denmark.

Det Frie Gymnasium,
Dambakken 9-11,
DK-3460 Birkerud,
Denmark.

Tvind Hogskole,
DK - 6990 Ulfborg,
Denmark.

France

Association Nouvelle Vague,
Chemin des Canotiers,
Ile Barthelasse,
84000 Avignon,
France.
(travelling school)

Graine d'Ecole,
La Paillerie,
Avenue de Bardenac,
33600 Pessac,
France.

International Travelling School,
9 Rue d'Argenteuil,
F-75001 Paris,
France.
tel: 331-42-60-4200

La Source, Ecole Nouvelle,
11 Rue Ernest Renan,
92190 Meudon Belle Oue,
France.

Oleron LEPMO,
St. Nazaire,
Paris,
France.

Theleme,
1 Rue des Nefliers,
31400 Toulouse,
France.

Germany

Freie Schule Bochum,
Kassenbergstrasse,
Bochum,
West Germany

Freie Schule Braunschweig,
Stettinstrasse 5,
Braunschweig,
West Germany

Freie Schule Frankfurt,
Vogelweidestrasse 3,
Frankfurt,
West Germany.

Freie Schule Marburg,
Grod-Seelheimstrasse 12,
Marburg,
West Germany.

Freie Schule Untertaunus,
Bruhlstrasse 11,
Aarbergen,
West Germany.

Glockseeschule,
A M Lindhofe 18,
Hanover,
West Germany.

Kinderschule Hamburg,
Altonaer Poststrasse 7,
Hamburg,
West Germany.

Wolf Eckhard Failling Comenius-Schule,
Rathausstrasse 7,
Darmstadt 12,
West Germany.

India

Maharaja Sawai Man Singh Vidyalaya,
Sawai Ram Singh Road,
Jaipur 302004,
India.

Japan

Chikyu no Kodomo no Ie,
(The Earth Kids' House),
2-51-7,
Tama-ma chi,
Huchu-shi,
Tokyo.
(about 20 5-18 year olds, established
1988)

Global Free School,
525-3 Imazu-Machi Takasago-Cho
Takasazo City,
Japan.

Nonami Kodomono Nura,
(Nonami Children's Village)
28-341 Nonami,
Tenpaku-cho,
Huchu-shi,
Tokyo,
Japan.
(a small nursery and primary school
influenced by the philosphy of AS Neill)

Nepal

Familial Day Nursery Kindergarten
School,
PO Box 2009,
Kathmandu,
Nepal.

New Zealand

Auckland Metropolitan,
16 Ngauruhoe Street,
PO Box 67-1-6,
Mt Eden,
Auckland,
New Zealand.

Four Avenues High School,
102 Champion Street,
Christchurch,
New Zealand.

Tamariki Free School,
83 Rutherford Street,
Box 19-506,
Christchurch,
New Zealand.

Thailand

The Children's Village School,
Tombol,
Wangdong,
Amphoe,
Muang,
Kanchanaburi,
71190,
Thailand.

U.S.A.

Albany Free School,
8 Elm Street,
Albany,
NY. 12202,

City as School,
16 Clarkson Street,
New York,
NY. 10014,

The Pilot School,
459 Broadway Street,
Cambridge,
MA. 0221 38,